Widowhood in Later Life

by

Anne Martin Matthews, Ph.D.

Director, Gerontology Research Centre
and Professor, Department of Family Studies
University of Guelph

Butterworths
Toronto and Vancouver

Widowhood in Later Life
© Butterworths Canada Ltd. 1991

Printed and bound in Canada by John Deyell Company

The Butterworth Group of Companies

Canada	Butterworths Canada Ltd., Toronto and Vancouver, 75 Clegg Road, MARKHAM, Ontario, L6G 1A1 and 409 Granville St., Ste. 1455, VANCOUVER, B.C., V6C 1T2
Australia	Butterworths Pty Ltd., SYDNEY, MELBOURNE, BRISBANE, ADELAIDE, PERTH, CANBERRA and HOBART
Ireland	Butterworths (Ireland) Ltd., DUBLIN
New Zealand	Butterworths of New Zealand Ltd., WELLINGTON and AUCKLAND
Puerto Rico	Equity de Puerto Rico, Inc., HATO REY
Singapore	Malayan Law Journal Pte. Ltd., SINGAPORE
United Kingdom	Butterworth & Co. (Publishers) Ltd., LONDON and EDINBURGH
United States	Butterworth Legal Publishers, AUSTIN, Texas; BOSTON, Massachusetts; CLEARWATER, Florida (D & S Publishers); ORFORD, New Hampshire (Equity Publishing); ST. PAUL, Minnesota; and SEATTLE, Washington

Canadian Cataloguing in Publication Data

Matthews, Anne Martin
   Widowhood in later life

(Perspectives on individual and population aging series)
Includes bibliographical references and index.
ISBN 0-409-88854-0

1. Widows – Social conditions. 2. Widowers – Social conditions. 3. Aged – Social conditions. I. Title.

HQ1058.M37   1991 305.26   C91-093383-9

Sponsoring Editor — Gloria Vitale
Development Editor — Edward O'Connor
Editor — Julia Keeler
Cover Design — Patrick Ng
Production — Kevin Skinner
Typesetting — McGraphics Desktop Publishing

To the memory of

Mary Pelma Victoria Erskine (née Fletcher)
May 24, 1901- January 14, 1987

who introduced me to the social world of widows.

Donated to

Augustana University College

by

FRANCIS   PUFFER

BUTTERWORTHS PERSPECTIVES ON INDIVIDUAL AND POPULATION AGING SERIES

This Series represents an exciting and significant development for the field of gerontology in Canada. The production of Canadian-based knowledge about individual and population aging is expanding rapidly, and students, scholars and practitioners are seeking comprehensive yet succinct summaries of the literature on specific topics. Recognizing the common need of this diverse community of gerontologists, Janet Turner, while she was Sponsoring Editor at Butterworths, conceived the idea of a series of specialized monographs that could be used in gerontology courses to complement existing texts and, at the same time, to serve as a valuable reference for those initiating research, developing policies, or providing services to elderly Canadians.

Each monograph includes a state-of-the-art review and analysis of the Canadian-based scientific and professional knowledge on the topic. Where appropriate for comparative purposes, information from other countries is introduced. In addition, some important policy and program implications of the current knowledge base are discussed, and unanswered policy and research questions are raised to stimulate further work in the area. The monographs are written for a wide audience: undergraduate students in a variety of gerontology courses; graduate students and research personnel who need a summary and analysis of the Canadian literature prior to initiating research projects; practitioners who are involved in the daily planning and delivery of services to aging adults; and policy-makers who require current and reliable information in order to design, implement and evaluate policies and legislation for an aging population.

The decision to publish a monograph on a specific topic is based in part on the relevance of the topic for the academic and professional community, as well as on the amount of information available at the time an author is signed to a contract. Because gerontology in Canada is attracting large numbers of highly qualified graduate students as well as increasingly active research personnel in academic, public and private settings, new areas of concentrated research are evolving. Future monographs will reflect this evolution of knowledge pertaining to individual or population aging in Canada.

Before introducing the thirteenth monograph in the Series, I would like, on behalf of the Series' authors and the gerontology community, to acknowledge the following members of the Butterworths "team" and their respective staff for their unique and sincere contribution to gerontology in Canada: Andrew Martin, President, for his continuing support of the Series; Craig Laudrum, Academic Acquisitions Manager, for his enthusiastic commitment to the promotion and expansion of the Series; and Linda Kee, Assistant Vice-President, Editorial, for her co-ordination of the editorial services. For each of you, we hope the knowledge provided in the Series will have personal value — but not until well into the next century!

Barry McPherson
Series Editor

FOREWORD

In the early years of gerontology, widowhood, like retirement, was primarily studied as an inevitable event in later life. Moreover, the two role transitions were often viewed as problems that led to stressful outcomes for the individual. Seldom was the impact of these two events considered from a societal perspective. More recently, however, like retirement, widowhood is being studied as a process rather than as a problem, and is being studied from the dual perspective of the individual and of society. Consequently, at the individual level of analysis, more research and policy attention is being focused on longer-term personal and interpersonal changes that result from the experience of being widowed, rather than on the initial period of mourning and grief management. Similarly, at the societal level of analysis, the focus is less on the stereotypical, normative role of the widowed in a society and more on such issues as the availability of, and access to, social support for the widowed; their economic and employment opportunities and status; the sociodemographic heterogeneity of the older widow and widower; the process of anticipatory socialization; and the status and the role of widowed persons in comparison with the never married, the separated, or the divorced.

The outcome of this shift from a problem to a process perspective, and from a focus on the immediate individual response to a longer-term analysis on both the individual and the societal levels is clearly summarized and analysed in this monograph. Written by the recognized Canadian expert on widowhood, the monograph fully develops and extends the brief discussions of the topic that were included in three earlier monographs in the Series: *Canada's Aging Population* (S. McDaniel); *Women and Aging* (E. Gee and M. Kimball); and *Family Ties and Aging* (I. Connidis).

While widowhood may be experienced by both genders at any age, over 80 percent of the 1.2 million widowed persons in Canada are women; and of this 80 percent, almost 75 percent are 65 years of age or older. More significantly, given such facts as the increasing sex ratio, the greater life expectancy of women, the tendency for women to marry older men, and the decreased likelihood that older women who are divorced or widowed will remarry, the average age at widowhood and the average duration of widowhood may increase further in the years ahead. Clearly, the onset of widowhood is one of the major factors contributing to the emergence of the view that "aging is a women's issue."

For most older women, while widowhood is an expectable life event, the onset occurs suddenly and unexpectedly. For this reason, the immediate response and adjustment are often stressful and traumatic. But, as Dr. Martin Matthews clearly demonstrates, in the long term, most women adjust and change in a positive direction once the bereavement process subsides and the reconstruction of a new identity and lifestyle begins. Some of these positive changes in identity, image, and lifestyle are vividly illustrated in this monograph through the use of insightful quotes reported by elderly, widowed respondents in two Canadian studies conducted by the author. In addition to the qualitative evidence presented in the quotations, the two studies also provide recent quantitative evidence to describe and explain the experience and the meaning of widowhood in the later years. Throughout the monograph, the symbolic interactionist perspective is employed wherever possible as the basis for examining the social-psychological processes associated with the long-term socialization and adaptation to the social world of the widowed. This in-depth review and analysis is structured around three general themes: adaptation (e.g., Chapters 2, 4, and 5); social support (e.g., Chapters 3, 4, and 5); and variability (e.g., Chapters 4 and 5). While the emphasis is on Canadian studies, comparisons and contrasts with the process and the outcome for the widowed in other countries are introduced as necessary.

Chapter 1 introduces the major issues to be addressed when studying widowhood in a Canadian context. Specifically, Dr. Martin Matthews presents current demographic realities and future projections for widowhood in later life, reviews the various conceptual and methodological approaches that can be employed to study this particular social world, and highlights the limitations of the existing research literature. A salient point arising from the demographic profile of older Canadians is that, despite increased divorce rates, the death of a spouse is still the typical way in which married life ends, and therefore a common life experience for most older women.

In Chapter 2, the literature pertaining to the processes of adjustment to this expectable life event is reviewed and critiqued. The subsections focus on socialization to the role of widowed person and the possibility of remarriage as a coping response. As well, the positive outcomes and the opportunities for personal growth and independence are stressed, and the myths of declining health and increased morbidity following widowhood are debunked.

The structure, sources, and processes of social support for older widows and widowers are reviewed in Chapter 3. This chapter begins with a brief overview of the concept and the measurement of social support (for a further discussion see the forthcoming monograph in this Series by Dr. N. Chappell, *Informal Support in Later Life*), and then describes the contribution of children, siblings, extended kin, friends and neighbours, self-help and mutual support groups, and formal support systems. In a unique contribution to the literature, the author discusses both the role of the deceased spouse as a continuing significant other, and the role of the self as a resource in the reconstruction of a new identity as widow or widower.

In Chapter 4 the considerable sociodemographic diversity of the older widowed population is highlighted. It is this heterogeneity that poses unique challenges to those seeking to provide either informal or formal support to the elderly widow or widower through social services or social policies. Specifically, variation by gender, urban versus rural residency, type of housing, parental status, ethnicity, cultural background, and financial resources are reviewed. Again, myths are shattered, especially with respect to economic status. In her discussion of financial resources, Dr. Martin Matthews introduces seldom-studied aspects of the financial status of elderly widows — the anxieties or uncertainties of managing money; and the fear, especially for long-living widows, that existing resources and anticipated income will be insufficient to economically survive in the years ahead.

Chapter 5 focuses on issues related to being single in later life, including a comparison of singlehood in later life for the widowed versus singlehood for the separated/divorced or never married. We learn that, contrary to conventional wisdom, the widowed are more similar to the never married in their use of support systems, but demonstrate quite different patterns of social support usage and levels of well-being than the separated/divorced older adult. This chapter also discusses the competing demands of working and/or caregiving that can detract from or enhance the process of adaptation to widowhood.

Chapter 6, as in the other monographs in the Series, raises many substantive, methodological, and policy questions that need to be addressed in the Canadian context. Taking an approach similar to that used by Professor Connidis in *Family Ties and Aging,* the author considers the social policy issues introduced in this monograph as either personal troubles or public issues, or both. In the past, widowhood has been viewed mostly as a personal trouble. But with the introduction of revisions to social security, family law, and pension legislation, widowhood has become more a societal responsibility that requires public policy initiatives and social service programs. To illustrate this trend, Dr. Martin Matthews describes some of the recent provincial and federal initiatives to enhance the quality of life of Canada's elderly widowed population.

In summary, this monograph provides the first in-depth examination of the research and policy literature on widowhood in Canada. For this reason, it should be read by students, practitioners, nurses, funeral home directors, social workers, researchers, policy makers, adult children, and the widowed. Throughout, we learn that after the early stage of grieving (one to two years), widowhood is not normally a period of stress and dependency for older Canadians. Rather, this role transition represents a period of personal change that can have both positive and negative outcomes. In reality, there are high levels of social support for those elderly widowed persons who need assistance at various stages of adaptation following the loss of a spouse. However, support services are not available everywhere or equally, and we do not understand all we should about this topic in a Canadian context. Therefore, further research and policy work are required, on both an individual and a societal level, especially with respect to ethnic and language groups, rural residents, lower-income groups, the employed older woman, widowers, and the very old who become widowed in their 70s or 80s. Widowhood is not a homogeneous experience or status, and increased effort is needed to understand more fully the diversity in responses and the diversity in subsequent lifestyles. Herein lies a challenge to those intrigued with the process whereby widowed persons adapt and maintain or change their self-identify as they negotiate and construct a new social identity and a new life as a single person.

Barry D. McPherson, Ph.D.
Series Editor
Wilfrid Laurier University
Waterloo, Ontario, Canada
February 1991

PREFACE

I came to the study of widowhood through a combination of academic purpose and serendipity. Many social scientists find that the questions which define their areas of academic interest derive from personal experience. I am no exception. As a graduate student I encountered regional and sociocultural differences in the process of relocating from one area of Canada to another. Consequently, I became interested in the social-psychological processes by which individuals who undergo major changes in their physical and social worlds adapt and are able to maintain their self-identity and negotiate a new meaning in their lives.

While I conducted my thesis research on Newfoundland migrants living in Hamilton, Ontario, and was immersed in the study of role transitions, I read David Sudnow's *Passing On: The Social Organization of Dying* (1967) as part of a graduate course. An ethnographic analysis of the social construction of death in the modern acute care hospital, this book represented for me a kind of "conversion," compelling me to look anew at a process I had previously thought of as inherently "physical." Sudnow's book prompted my interest in the experience of death from the perspective of the survivor. This research interest developed at a time when I was renting a flat in the home of an elderly childless widow, and thus had many opportunities to observe and to be a part of her social world and that of her widowed friends. Thus, I came to apply my interest in the role transitions associated with migration to the role transitions and social worlds associated with the elderly widowed, an interest that has shaped the past 15 years of my academic career.

The purpose of this monograph is to examine the experience of widowhood in later life through the integration of original Canadian data with existing research findings from the United States and other international sources. The focus is on the longer-term features of the social worlds of the widowed, rather than on the process of adaptation to bereavement *per se*. The social world of the widowed is examined within the context of three broad themes: adaptation, social support, and variability. Adaptation is examined in terms of socialization to the role of widowed person and in terms of the influence of competing role demands and housing environments in long-term adaptation to widowhood. The examination of social support focuses on the patterns of reciprocal exchange between the widowed and members of their formal and informal support systems, including family, friends, and neighbours. The consideration of variability in the experience of widowhood in later life focuses on comparisons and contrasts between women and men, between the rural and the urban widowed, and between the widowed with children and those without children. In addition, marital status comparisons are drawn between the widowed, the separated/divorced, and the never-married elderly in order to identify those aspects of being "unattached" in later life that are unique to the widowed. The monograph ends with an examination of how societal trends and public policies contribute to the variability of widowhood in later life.

ACKNOWLEDGEMENTS

Over the course of 15 years, since my first research with the widowed, many individuals have supported and encouraged the research on which this monograph is based. Helena Znaniecka Lopata of Loyola University in Chicago and Victor Marshall of the University of Toronto have both been particularly instrumental in nurturing this research interest, and I thank them sincerely. The Research Board at the University of Guelph provided funding for my first pilot study. The Social Sciences and Humanities Research Council of Canada funded several research projects on which this monograph draws: Grants #429-79-0017 Economic and Social Welfare of the Recently Retired (with Kathleen H. Brown); #492-84-0028 Rural-urban Comparisons of the Social Supports of the Widowed Elderly; #451-86-1254 Leave Fellowship; and #492-86-0022 The Never Married in Later Life (with Joan E. Norris).

I am grateful to Barry McPherson, the Series Editor, for his encouragement and support throughout this project, and to the acquisitions and editorial staff of Butterworths for their assistance and patience in working with an author who continually had too many competing role demands. Carol Harvey reviewed the manuscript and made numerous helpful suggestions.

I would like to thank the following for their permission to excerpt selected material which I have previously published:

> Duke University Press, Durham, N.C., for permission to publish excerpts from "Support Systems of Widows in Canada," pp. 225-50 in H.Z. Lopata (ed.), *Widows*. Vol. 2, *North America*. These excerpts appear on pp. 2-3, 10-12, 110-13, 117-18. Reprinted with the permission of the publisher, Duke University Press.

> Fitzhenry and Whiteside, Toronto, for permission to publish excerpts from "Widowhood as an Expectable Life Event," pp. 343-66 in V.W. Marshall (ed.), *Aging in Canada: Social Perspectives* (2d ed.). These excerpts appear on pp. 17-18, 19-20, 44-45, 51, and 63-66.

> *Journal of Rural Health* for permission to publish excerpts from "Social Supports of the Rural Widowed Elderly," 4(3): 57-70. These excerpts appear on pp. 73-78.

I am grateful to the Minister of Supply and Services in Ottawa for permission to reproduce, in the tables in Chapter 1, material taken from the following sources:

Statistics Canada (1982), *Population: Age, Sex and Marital Status.* 1981 Census of Canada, Catalogue No. 92-901. Table 3: Population by marital status and sex, for Canada and Provinces 1921-1981, p. 3-1. The material appears in Table 1.1, p. 3.

Statistics Canada (1987), *Population Age, Sex and Marital Status.* 1986 Census of Canada, Catalogue No. 93-901. Table 5: Population by selected age groups and sex, showing marital status. The material appears in Table 1.1 (p. 3) and Table 1.3 (p. 6).

L. Stone and H. Frenken, *Canada's Seniors*, Catalogue No. 98-121, p. 41. The material appears in Table 1.2, p. 5.

Many colleagues in Canada, the U.S., Britain, and Australia provided information on their research and I am grateful for their input and assistance. My colleague and friend Ingrid Connidis of the University of Western Ontario generously gave of her time in discussing the data and commenting on drafts, and commiserated warmly throughout the writing process. I thank her most sincerely. I also thank a number of individuals affiliated with the University of Guelph: Lucille Dickinson, Joanne Duncan-Robinson, Kim Eveleigh, Marlene Oatman, Lynda Ross, and Suzanne Wakefield all worked in the collection or the analysis of the data reported here; Betty Ware typed and retyped many drafts with much-appreciated expertise and great patience, all the while professing to actually enjoy it!

Time taken away from one's spouse to write a book about widowhood has a special irony to it, and I thank my husband, Ralph Matthews, for his understanding when the writing faltered or took longer than expected, for his unwavering support, and for cooperative sharing on the domestic front. I thank Adam and Leah for their gentle respect for their mother's need to spend time in her study, an activity that seems to have occupied much of their young lives. Max and Tess Martin experienced several disrupted family vacations while I wrote, and I am ever grateful for their interest and support.

This book is dedicated to the memory of my good friend "Mrs. E." When I rented rooms in her house in 1971, she quickly incorporated me into her social world of widows. The memories of those years, and the recollections of our many telephone conversations and hours in her parlour over a cup of tea, have shaped many of my interpretations and insights throughout these pages.

CONTENTS

TABLES

CHAPTER 1

APPROACHES TO THE STUDY OF WIDOWHOOD

INTRODUCTION

The scientific study of the experience of widowhood is a relatively recent development. Although there are historical accounts of cultural practices surrounding bereavement and mourning, and analyses of images of widowhood in folklore, drama, and history (Bensel-Myers 1985), only in the last 30 years have researchers and clinicians turned their attention to the systematic study of the personal adaptations and life changes coincident with the loss of the spouse. The major pioneering study of the widowed is Peter Marris's 1958 account of the social, financial, and emotional problems faced by young widows. In the North American context, significant research on widowhood appeared for the first time with the publication of Helena Znaniecka Lopata's *Widowhood in an American City* (1973b). In Canada, there is no research comparable to Lopata's studies in the United States. This monograph represents the first effort to synthesize Canadian studies of the widowed, and to compare and contrast this knowledge with the many U.S., British, and other studies of bereavement and widowhood.

Two historical trends have contributed to the emergence of scientific studies of widowhood. The first is the demographic pattern of population aging, with associated increases in the numbers of widowed persons in the population. The second is the feminist movement, with its imperative to examine life events and circumstances of particular concern to women, and to consider how societal norms and values contribute to the uniqueness of these experiences for women.

Much of the scientific interest in widowhood may be cast in two broad frameworks: studies that focus on the psychological processes of coping and adapting to loss and change, particularly in the early period of widowhood; and studies that focus on the social process of role transition associated with the movement from being a member of a couple to being "unattached." Rubenstein (1986) describes these as the intrapsychic and social-psychological aspects of widowhood. The overall orientation of this monograph is social-psychological. The perspective is that of a sociologist exploring the interaction between individuals and society as those indi-

1

viduals experience role transitions associated with both widowhood and aging. The examination of the demographic profile of widowhood in Canada, and the conceptual approaches that have characterized the study of widowhood, help set the context for this analysis.

DEMOGRAPHIC REALITIES

Patterns of widowhood in Canada have been characterized by both stability and profound change in recent years. In 1986, there were 1,250,395 widowed persons in Canada, representing 6 percent of the population aged 15 and over. This proportion has remained the same for the entire twentieth century. There has also been relatively little alteration in the long-term sex-specific nature of widowhood in Canada. At the time of the 1986 census, only 2 percent of males aged 15 and over were widowed, while 10 percent of women were (Statistics Canada 1987).

There have, however, been dramatic changes in the median age of the widowed and in the duration and age of onset of widowhood. Two factors now characterize the incidence of widowhood in the Canadian population: widowhood is sex-selective and is age-related. Eighty-three percent of the widowed are women, a proportion that has increased in recent decades. Among all ages in 1971, widows outnumbered widowers by nearly four to one. By 1981, the proportion had increased to almost five to one (Statistics Canada 1982), and it remained at this level in the 1986 census (Statistics Canada 1987; 1989). It is estimated that half of all marriages end with the death of the husband and only one-fifth end with the death of the wife (Statistics Canada 1988). Because of this demographic reality, discussions of widowhood generally focus on women; and because women predominate among the widowed, the generic pronoun "she" is used, when appropriate, throughout this book.

McDaniel's *Canada's Aging Population* (1986), another volume in this Series, indicated that most of the widowed are women because of the differential life expectancy of males and females. Another reason is the mating gradient, whereby husbands are generally two to three years older than their wives. Yet another factor that influences not only the likelihood of being widowed but also the numbers of widowed men and women in the population at any one point in time is the differential in rates of remarriage for widows and widowers. Not only are men far less likely to *become* widowed, but they are also less likely than women to *remain* widowed. While 14 percent of widowed men remarry, only 5 percent of widowed women do so (Statistics Canada 1988). For all age groups, widowers are four and one-half times more likely than widows to remarry. Among the population aged 70 and over, widowers are approximately nine times more likely to remarry than are widows (Northcott 1984). As a result of these factors, the relative proportions of male and female widowed in this country are quite different.

This difference has increased with each decade, although there is some recent evidence that the trend has started to slow somewhat.

In examining trends over time in the prevalence of widowhood in society, data can be analysed in two ways. One way is to consider changes in the absolute numbers of elderly widows and widowers. This kind of analysis is useful in the consideration of the demand for programmes and services targeted specifically to the widowed population. The second method of analysis involves the examination of change in the proportion of widowed persons relative to other marital status groups among the aged. This method contributes much to the development of policy by providing an overall demographic context in which to interpret patterns of marital status change. In order that trends in the prevalence of widowhood over the past 30 years can be understood, changes in both absolute numbers and relative proportions of the elderly widowed in the population will now be discussed.

As Table 1.1 illustrates, from 1961 to 1986 there was a substantial increase in the numbers of widows and widowers aged 65 and over in the Canadian population. However, the increase in the number of widows has far exceeded that of widowers. Between 1961 and 1986, the absolute numbers of elderly widowers increased by almost 12 percent. There were 16,098 more elderly widowed men in Canada in 1986 than in 1961. However, the absolute numbers of elderly widows increased in the same period by 117 percent. There were 407,017 more elderly widows in 1986 than in 1961. The

TABLE 1.1

PREVALENCE OF WIDOWS AND WIDOWERS AGED 65 YEARS AND OVER, CANADA, 1961, 1971, 1981, AND 1986

	Widowers	Widows
1961	137,277	346,903
1971	130,235	475,635
1981	142,820	662,210
1986	153,375	753,920
Percent Change 1961-1971*	– 9.5%	+ 37.1%
Percent Change 1971-1981*	+ 9.7%	+ 39.2%
Percent Change 1981-1986*	+ 7.4%	+ 13.8%
Percent Change 1961-1986*	+ 11.7%	+ 117.3%

* Percentage calculations are by Martin Matthews.

SOURCE: Statistics Canada (1982). *Population: Age, Sex and Marital Status.* 1981 Census of Canada, Catalogue No. 92–901. Table 3: Population by marital status and sex, for Canada and Provinces 1921–1981, p. 3–1 (Ottawa: Minister of Supply and Services). Reproduced with permission.

Statistics Canada (1987). *Population: Age, Sex and Marital Status.* 1986 Census of Canada, Catalogue No. 93–901. Table 5: Population by selected age groups and sex, showing marital status (Ottawa: Minister of Supply and Services). Reproduced with permission.

data in Table 1.1 further indicate that the rate of growth in the numbers of elderly widowed in the population has been somewhat slower in the 1980s than in the two previous decades. For example, there were only 14 percent more elderly widows between 1981 and 1986, compared with an increase of 39 percent between 1971 and 1981.

The reduced rate of growth in the widowed population aged 55 to 64 (not shown in Table 1.1) is particularly striking. The numbers of widowed women aged 55 to 64 increased by 27 percent between 1961 and 1971; increased a further 18 percent between 1971 and 1981; but essentially stabilized (showing a *decrease* of .001 percent) between 1981 and 1986. A substantial decrease in the numbers of widowed women in the aged 55 to 59 cohort accounts for this overall stabilizing effect. For men, the pattern of growth is different. The number of widowed men aged 55 to 64 decreased by 11 percent between 1961 and 1971; increased by 9 percent between 1971 and 1981; and increased again by 7 percent between 1981 and 1986.

While the examination of absolute numbers of the widowed elderly emphasizes the growth in this population in recent years, the analysis of proportional or relative change presents a rather different picture. One such analysis calculates a "widowhood ratio" by considering the proportion of widowed people among those who have ever been married (Stone and Frenken 1988). An examination of census data shows that between 1976 and 1986 the widowhood ratio for individuals aged 65 and over declined from 55 percent to 53 percent for women and from 17 percent to 15 percent for men. This decrease in the widowhood ratio is an extension of a downward trend first observed around 1966 (Stone and Frenken 1988). While this trend is most pronounced among the 65 to 69 age group, even among women aged 75 to 79 the widowhood ratio has dropped from 66 percent in 1966 to 62 percent in 1986.

The data presented in Table 1.2 reflect yet another way of understanding change in the patterns of widowhood over time. These data indicate that the rate of growth for widowhood is lower than for most other marital statuses, and that for women there has been a notable decline in average annual rates of growth of widowhood in the past 15 years. It appears that reductions in the mortality rates of older men are beginning to have an impact on the incidence of widowhood among women now entering old age. Stone and Fletcher (1986, 3.1) reported a 14 percent decline in the death rate for men aged 50 to 54 between 1976 and 1981. They noted that "all the older age categories of men recorded mortality declines of 6 percent or more during that time."

Table 1.3 illustrates the proportions of each age group who were widowed at the time of the 1986 census of Canada. When compared with data from the 1981 census, these proportions either remained the same or declined very slightly over the five-year period (Devereaux 1988, 26). Overall, the proportion of widowed men in the adult population remained

TABLE 1.2

AVERAGE ANNUAL GROWTH RATES OF THE OLDER POPULATION BY MARITAL STATUS AND SEX, CANADA, 1976–1981 AND 1981–1986

Age Group, Sex, and Marital Status	Average Annual Growth Rate	
	1976–1981	1981–1986
	%	%
Aged 65 and Over		
Males:		
Married/Separated	3.6	2.7
Single	0.5	– 0.1
Widowed	**1.4**	**1.5**
Divorced	14.1	8.3
Total	3.1	2.4
Females:		
Married/Separated	4.5	3.8
Single	2.3	1.0
Widowed	**3.6**	**2.8**
Divorced	15.8	12.1
Total	4.0	3.2

SOURCE: L. Stone and H. Frenken (1988). *Canada's Seniors*. Catalogue No. 98-121, p. 41, based on census data (Ottawa: Minister of Supply and Services). Reproduced with permission.

stable in this period (2 percent in both 1981 and 1986) and the proportion of widowed women increased very slightly between 1981 and 1986.

The discussion thus far has focused on the sex-selective nature of widowhood in Canada. The age-related nature of widowhood is also illustrated in Table 1.3. In recent decades the average age at widowhood has steadily increased, with the proportion of the widowed in each age cohort rising dramatically from age 50 onward. Widowhood in Canada is associated not only with women, but now also with the elderly. On the average, women now become widowed at age 69 and men become widowed at age 73 (Statistics Canada 1988). Almost three-quarters (73 percent) of widows in Canada are over the age of 65. The average age of the widowed population is 75 years for both men and women (Statistics Canada 1988). In the 65-and-over age group, 48 percent of women and 14 percent of men are widowed; in the aged-80-and-over group, this proportion rises to 74 percent of women and 32 percent of men (Stone and Frenken 1988).

Two other issues are of relevance to a discussion of the demography of widowhood. The first involves the expectability of widowhood as a life event, and the second the relative duration of widowhood in the lives of the elderly. Because most Canadians marry, the experience of widowhood is an

TABLE 1.3

WIDOWED POPULATION AGED 15 YEARS AND OVER,
BY SEX AND AGE COHORTS, CANADA, 1986

		Widowers		Widows
	N	Percentage of Age Cohort*	N	Percentage of Age Cohort*
Total, 15 + Years	210,880	2.2	1,039,520	10.2
15–19	315	0.03	605	0.06
20–24	420	0.04	1,090	0.10
25–29	620	0.05	2,645	0.22
30–34	1,170	0.11	5,380	0.49
35–39	2,125	0.21	9,450	0.93
40–44	3,130	0.39	14,765	1.8
45–49	4,780	0.72	23,110	3.5
50–54	8,360	1.4	40,260	6.6
55–59	14,680	2.5	72,010	11.8
60–64	21,915	4.1	116,275	19.6
65–69	26,920	6.5	149,750	30.1
70–74	33,420	10.3	175,800	42.5
75–79	34,135	16.3	167,760	55.8
80–84	29,190	25.3	132,690	68.4
85–89	18,535	38.2	81,515	78.7
90 +	11,175	54.0	46,405	84.4

* Percentage calculations are by Martin Matthews.
SOURCE: Statistics Canada (1987). *Population: Age, Sex and Marital Status.* 1986 Census of Canada, Catalogue No. 93–901. Table 5: Population by selected age groups and sex, showing marital status (Ottawa: Minister of Supply and Services). Reproduced with permission.

"expectable" event of later life for most people. For 70 percent of marriages, partners remain together " 'til death do us part" (Statistics Canada 1988). Although the Canadian divorce rate has nearly doubled since a *Divorce Act* was legislated in 1968 (S.C. 1967-68, c. 24), the current rate of 1125.2 divorces per 100,000 married women aged 15 years and over (Statistics Canada 1985b, 10) still remains about half the U.S. rate. The high annual growth rate among the divorced elderly population, as depicted in Table 1.2, reflects not so much the rate at which the elderly are terminating their marriages as it does "the number of persons who arrived in the 'senior category' as divorced persons" (Stone and Frenken 1988, 39). For the near future, the death of the spouse will be the typical end to the married life of Canadians.

Because Canadian women tend, on the average, to marry men who are two and one-half years older than themselves, and because of the longer life expectancy of women, the average length of widowhood for women is almost twice that of men. Among men, the average length of widowhood has increased slightly from 7.8 years in 1970-1972 to 8.1 years in 1984-1986. Among women, the average length of widowhood increased from 14.5 years in 1970-1972 to 15.4 years in 1984-1986 (Statistics Canada 1988).

Differences in life expectancy between men and women are expected to increase in the future (McDaniel 1986). While widows make up over half of the population over age 65, widowers make up approximately only 20 percent of this age group. Projections are that the number of widows in the older Canadian population will grow by 36 percent between 1975 and 2000. Among women over the age of 75 the number of widowed is expected to grow by 100 percent. As McDaniel notes (1986, 117), "the differential life expectancy of men and women, combined with changing family structure and women's lesser economic independence, means that careful attention should be directed to the needs of widows."

CONCEPTUAL APPROACHES TO THE STUDY OF WIDOWHOOD

This demographic analysis of the prevalence of widowhood in Canadian society indicates that widowhood is a status held by many aged individuals, and most elderly women. However, widowhood is a *process* as well as a *status* (Troll et al. 1979, 79). Consequently, it is appropriate that studies of widowhood focus on both short-term and long-term effects. Most people who are widowed remain so for a considerable portion of their lives. The transition from married to widowed person is one that calls for many long-term changes in identity and the reorganization of social roles.

Relatively little Canadian research has been completed on widowhood as a process of transition. Canadian studies that examine patterns of social support in widowhood, for example, primarily focus on the supportive relationships of those who currently hold the status of "widowed person." Few studies have examined the way in which social relationships and support systems are changed by the process of becoming widowed. For such analyses, longitudinal research is required. The research findings reported in this monograph are based primarily on small cross-sectional studies. These have typically examined the what and how of the reconstructed social world in widowhood, but not the actual process of reconstruction. In both Canada and the United States, research that more fully addresses the social meaning of widowhood for men and women is quite rare. As one participant in a study of widowhood noted, "Maybe the why of things should have been asked more often. Circumstances can change the meaning of answers to some of the questions" (Lopata 1979, 367). Where possible throughout this monograph, the *why* of men's and women's experiences of widowhood is emphasized. This orientation to the study of widowhood reflects a symbolic interactionist framework that considers individuals as active creators of their social worlds. As Gee and Kimball

(1987, 7) noted in *Women and Aging*, another volume in this Series, the application of symbolic interactionism to the study of later life "focuses primarily on how older individuals interpret and give meaning to events and situations in their lives."

This orientation is not an easy one to apply to the study of widowhood, since much of the research is essentially atheoretical, "issue-related, descriptive work" (Gee and Kimball 1987, 10). This characteristic of widowhood research is not atypical of research on women and aging in general. "Too much of the research on women and aging is descriptive, lacking any explicit theoretical basis... We know many facts; we are more than ready for theoretical integration and refinement" (Gee and Kimball 1987, 108).

While widowhood research is largely atheoretical, many studies fall within a framework based on a role theory model of women and aging. The social role is seen as a set of functionally interdependent, patterned relations between a social person and the participants in her social circle. This role consists of her duties and the personal rights that those duties grant her in order that she may be able to carry out her part (Lopata 1973b, 2).

Role theory is the theoretical framework of several major studies of widowhood (Lopata 1973b; 1979). Other studies of widowhood are couched in similar terms, conceptualizing widowhood as a role loss (Cumming and Henry 1961) or as a form of role exit (Blau 1973). These studies analyse bereavement in terms of role change, from the role of wife to the role of widow. This perspective conceptualizes role exit as the cessation of any stable pattern of interaction and shared activities between two or more persons. The experience of bereavement in widowhood is caused not only by the death itself but also by the termination of an enduring pattern of activity between one person and a significant other (Blau 1973, 210).

Within this perspective, widowhood in later life represents a "terminal" role exit, a permanent detachment of the individual from participation in family life. Such a view considers widowhood to be a "roleless status" lacking any culturally prescribed rights and duties towards others in the social system (Blau 1973, 13). Role loss, a term frequently used in the literature on old age to refer to such life events as retirement and widowhood, emphasizes the involuntary character of these experiences. Within this perspective, the fundamental conceptual construct is the role, with the focus primarily on loss. Issues of identity change and the negotiation of self-concept are typically not addressed in this body of research. There is ample empirical evidence that, for the cohorts of women now in old age, social identity was typically derived through the husband's occupation and that at his death such women were compelled to reconstruct their self-concept. However, widowhood research, based largely on a role theory perspective, has generally not addressed issues of identity change with widowhood. Lopata is among the few to link role loss and identity change in her research. She notes that "many widows consider the role of wife to have been a very important one, and the difficulties involved in losing this identity are compounded by the fact that most widows lack another major role upon which to now focus a new identity" (Lopata 1973b, 92).

But beyond this, most research on widowhood fails to consider the extent to which "typical" responses to widowhood (such as disbelief, loss of a sense of reality, despondency, and idealization of the husband's memory) relate not only to the loss of the spouse, but also to the loss of a primary source of identity for many women now in old age. Because of this failure, we have little understanding of many of the unique features of the experience of widowhood. These include sanctifying the late spouse's memory, experiencing obsessive thoughts of him, and imagining him present. Whether these are affected not only by the widow's longing for her spouse as a unique individual but also by her need to preserve the continuity of her own sense of self is not yet well understood. Nor has the literature fully explored the issue of whether these experiences are more characteristic of widows than of widowers. The widow's loss of her primary source of identity and presumably (although not always) her most significant "significant other" is typically considered in most widowhood studies only in terms of the roleless status of the bereaved.

A symbolic interactionist approach is better able to ascertain the basis of responses to bereavement and widowhood and to account for factors that role theory cannot adequately consider. Role theory, as defined by Parsons and Merton, has been challenged on the grounds that it conceives of role performance as a form of behavioural conformity to expectations in order to receive positive sanctions from those holding these expectations, or to avoid negative sanctions (McCall and Simmons 1966, 6). It is only in highly ritualistic relations that the direction and content of conduct can be prescribed in this manner by roles (Blumer 1969, 75). Because there is no set "script" for most role relationships, incumbents are continually required to "improvise their roles" within broadly defined limits (McCall and Simmons 1966, 7).

Role definitions thus become "creative compromises" (Turner 1962, 32), and role theory therefore concerns itself with how such compromises are achieved. Instead of considering the multitude of possible relationships between the roles of self and "other," role theorists generally focus primarily on the pattern of conformity between roles. A further shortcoming of this approach, characteristic of the widowhood literature, is the tendency of role theory to be strongly negative. Often it deals only with the malfunctioning or lack of functioning of roles in role conflict, role loss, and roleless status, and avoids the issue of how roles function under normal circumstances (Turner 1962, 21). Role, therefore, becomes an inadequate explanation of what transpires in interaction. Thus, we must shift our emphasis away from role theory to the methods individuals employ to devise their interaction.

The theory of symbolic interaction takes as its central problem: How is it possible for collective human action to occur? How is it possible for people to adjust their actions to those of others in such a way as to make collective acts possible? Mead (1964) and his followers utilized such concepts as meaning, symbols, taking the role of the other, society, and self to explain how our ways of thinking about our world and acting in it change as the others with whom we interact change themselves or are replaced (Becker 1970, 290). Changes in the self derive from continual adjustments in the person's notions of how others will respond to her actions, and from the meaning she gives to her own actions based on the earlier responses of others.

From the standpoint of symbolic interactionism, social roles merely set the conditions for individual interaction, but they do not determine action. The role enters into action "...only to the extent to which it shapes situations in which people act, ...[and] supplies fixed sets of symbols which people use in interpreting their situations" (Blumer 1969, 88). Between initiating factors and the action that may follow in their wake, Mead interjects a process of self-interaction. Mead's concepts of the "I" and the "me" are relevant to this analysis. Put simply, the I is the response of the organism to the attitudes of others; the me is the organized set of attitudes of others that one herself assumes. The attitudes of others comprise the organized me, and then one acts toward that as an I (Mead 1964, 230). The individual thus becomes a part of her own experience as an object, not as a subject. Only on the basis of social relations and interactions can she become that object (Mead 1964, 244).

Throughout this monograph, the transition to widowhood is conceptualized from the perspective of symbolic interactionism. Within this framework, it is not change in role that forms the basis of identity change. Rather, it is the redefinition — of the attitudes of others, and ensuingly, of the me — that accounts for such change. Approached in this way, widowhood (paraphrasing Berger and Kellner's description of marriage) is regarded as "...involving not only stepping into new roles, but, beyond this, stepping into a new world" (Berger and Kellner 1970, 67). The process of self-interaction thus requires the widow to meet and handle her world through a redefining process instead of by merely responding to it, "and forces her to construct her action instead of merely releasing it" (Blumer 1969, 63).

RESEARCHING THE WIDOWHOOD EXPERIENCE

While there is now a growing body of Canadian research on women in widowhood, in contrast with the situation only a decade ago (Martin Matthews 1980b), this area of research is still very much in its infancy. Most current and completed research falls into one of three classifications: studies focused on temporal dimensions of the process of adjusting to bereavement; studies on correlates of the status of widowhood itself; and studies on the post-grieving period of later widowhood, when issues of the reconstruction of one's identity and social world become salient. These studies focus primarily on women's experiences of widowhood, with very little research examining the circumstances of widowers.

The focus of the first type of research is on the process of adaptation to bereavement, which covers a period of time up to approximately two years after the death of the spouse. Haas-Hawkings, et al. (1985), for example, examined patterns of relatively immediate psychosocial adjustment to widowhood (4 to 12 weeks after the loss). They found positive correlations between preparation for loss and self-report of adjustment. Other research at the Clarke Institute of Psychiatry in Toronto has also focused on the bereavement process, and is unique in Canada because of its longitudinal design. Studies by Vachon and her colleagues examined the widow's situation at 1 month, 6 months, 12, and 24 months after the death of the spouse. Reports on this comprehensive research (Vachon et al. 1976; Vachon, et al. 1977; Walker et al. 1977; and Vachon 1981) indicate that bereavement typically alters patterns of interaction with significant others, frequently in association with high levels of stress. The research of Haas-Hawkings et al. and Vachon and associates thus exemplifies a type of investigation that deals with the more immediate or short-term consequences of the bereavement experience, with the focus primarily on adjustment as the outcome.

A second body of research on the widowed in Canada considers the characteristics of older widowed women in a variety of settings. Here the focus is on the correlates of the status of widowhood itself. Christiansen-Ruffman (1976, 457) has observed that frequently in social science "concepts such as age and sex... simply characterize the individual but ignore the social meaning given to these characteristics in a particular setting." In this second type of research, investigations are made of elderly individuals, most of them women, who happen also to be widowed. Such research contributes substantially to our knowledge of the characteristics of widowed persons, but does not focus on the issue of the social meaning of the status of widow.

Examples of this kind of research include provincial government profiles of the correlates of the widowed status for both women and men. One such study identifies low income as the major problem for women, and social isolation as the major problem for men (Saskatchewan Senior Citizens' Provincial Council 1979). Federally sponsored projects include a report on the living arrangements of older women in Canada, most of whom are widowed (Fletcher and Stone 1980) and a joint federal-provincial project identifying elderly widowed females who live alone as accounting for one in five of all admissions to home care programs (Health and Welfare Canada 1982, 16).

In the third classification are those studies of the later widowhood period (usually four or more years after bereavement) where the focus of analysis shifts from adaptation *per se* to the examination of the reconstructed social world and the identity and social meaning of the status of widow. This type of research reflects a recent trend among social gerontologists "to conceptualize widowhood as a life-course transition that has implications far beyond the death of one's spouse" (Markides and Cooper 1989, 3). To date, much of this research is generally cross-sectional and frequently comparative in design. For example, Stryckman's (1981b) analysis of the decision to remarry compares the attitudes and social circumstances of elderly remarried and widowed men and women. It focuses on the social meaning that potential or actual remarriage has for the widowed and their kin relationships. Similarly, Norris (1980) examines the characteristics of the social personality of elderly widows as contrasted with those of never-married older women. Her data indicate widows' ongoing involvement in and emotional commitment to the role of wife long after the death of the spouse. Another example is a study of the support systems of women widowed five to ten years (Martin Matthews 1982), as well as research on rural-urban comparisons of the social supports of widows and widowers (Martin Matthews 1988a; 1988b). These research projects will be discussed more fully throughout this monograph.

LIMITATIONS OF EXISTING RESEARCH

While the aging of the population in Canada is well documented and widely acknowledged, the implications of old age for the experience of widowhood are not always recognized. Table 1.2 illustrates the extent to which widowhood is age-related. Although widowhood is a characteristic feature of later life, and particularly late old age, most studies have focused on younger populations. For example, among some of the best-known studies of widowhood, Glick et al.'s (1974) research is based on a sample of widowed persons aged 45 or younger; Lopata's (1973b) sample included individuals over 65, but 81 percent of the study group had been widowed prior to age 65; Morgan's (1976) sample was aged 45 to 74; and in Bankoff's (1983a; 1983b) research, the mean age of the widowed was 51 years.

Relatively few studies extensively examine issues specific to elderly widows. These include the work of Gibbs (1979), whose respondents ranged from age 55 to 94, with a mean age of about 75; Arling (1976), whose sample was aged 65 and over; and Scott and Kivett (1980), whose sample age range was 65 to 99 years. One major study to focus on the elderly population surveyed the widowed aged 65 and over (Lopata 1979).

In Canadian research virtually nothing is known about older widowed persons. For example, Vachon and her associates have focused primarily on widowed populations aged 22 to 69 (Vachon 1981) and aged 55 to 69 (Vachon et al. 1977). Haas-Hawkings et al. (1985) studied a group ranging in age from 49 to 83, with a mean age of 66. Norris (1980) studied a group of women who had been widowed for ten years and whose average age was 70 to 71, but the sample size was only 11. Stryckman (1982) reported only that her sample of widowed were "all at least 55 or over," although she did report the average age at widowhood as 62.8.

Widowhood research has persisted in its focus on younger age groups, despite the aging of the population and the increasing proportions of those aged 80 and over (Health and Welfare Canada 1983), the vast majority of whom are widowed. This focus on the younger widowed also belies the fact that age is a critical feature of the widowhood experience. Although empirical support for this relationship has primarily emerged in studies of women, there is reason to believe that it applies to widowers as well.

In research on widows, Lopata found that "...the age at which the wife experiences the death of her husband is a very important feature of widowhood because of the way her life is immersed in other social roles" (1973b, 33). Further,

> the widow's age at the time she becomes widowed...and at various junctures afterwards, is a major factor affecting the impact of the community's institutional opportunity structure for reconstructing social life because age serves as an eligibility criteria for participation in, or exclusion from, various social institutions within the community... In addition to formal eligibility requirements, age serves in a number of non-formalized ways to define normative expectations and behaviors. [Gibbs 1979, 14]

Throughout this monograph, the primary focus is on the experience of widowhood in later life. Where appropriate, comparative data are presented on younger age groups of women and men who are widowed, particularly in mid-life. The experience of widowhood among those younger than age 50 is non-normative and relatively rare, and as a life event will vary considerably from the patterns described here. Research findings on younger widowed persons are reported here only as they provide a counterpoint to the discussion of the circumstances of those widowed in later life.

STRUCTURE OF THE MONOGRAPH

Three broad themes characterize the examination of widowhood in Canada throughout this monograph: adaptation, social support, and variability. The theme of adaptation is emphasized most particularly in Chapter 2, in the context of discussions of socialization to the role of widowed person, coping mechanisms in bereavement, health outcomes, and the option of remarriage. It emerges again in Chapter 5 in the consideration of competing role demands such as retirement and caregiving, and in Chapter 4 in analyses of how housing environment may influence long-term adaptation to widowhood.

The concept of social support guides the analysis of the experience of widowhood in Chapters 3, 4, 5. Chapter 3 focuses on the pattern of reciprocal exchanges of social support between the widowed and members of their informal and formal support systems, measured in terms of social, emotional, service, and financial support. Chapter 4 compares levels of support between different groups of widowed persons, for example, men versus women, rural versus urban. In Chapter 5, specific comparisons are made between the social supports available to the widowed and to other "unattached" elderly, the separated/divorced, and the never married.

The issue of variability in the experience of widowhood also pervades this monograph, but is most specifically dealt with in Chapters 4 and 5. In another monograph in this Series, *Women and Aging*, Gee and Kimball (1987, 108) decry the fact that "there has been very little work concerned with *variations* among women in any of the issues we have discussed. A basic tenet of theory-building and theory-testing is that variations should be examined." While they note that "in this body of research literature the variations that are studied are those comparing women and men" (ibid.), they call for comparative research that focuses on such dimensions as ethnic differences in women's aging, rural/urban, regional, social class, and marital status comparisons.

> A focus on variations, which in our opinion is the largest gap in the existing literature, will not only open the door for theoretical insights and refinements, but will also represent a major step in dismantling the largely implicit assumption that women are a homogeneous group in society who experience aging, both objectively and subjectively, in a similar fashion. [Gee and Kimball 1987, 109]

It is equally true that the widowed, and particularly the female widowed, are frequently treated in the literature as a homogeneous group. In order to dispel this image and to contribute to theory building within the study of widowhood, a major portion of this volume deals with the issue of variability between women and men, between the rural and the urban widowed, between older and younger widowed, and between the widowed with and without children in their experience of this particular life event. In addition, in order to understand which aspects of being an "unattached" person in later life are unique to the widowed, marital status comparisons are drawn between the widowed, separated/divorced, and never-married elderly. The final chapter takes a broader macro-sociological approach in examining the ways in which societal trends, such as birth rates and labour force participation rates of women, and policies related to public and private pensions and the *Canadian Charter of Rights and Freedoms* (enacted as Schedule B to the *Canada Act, 1982* (U.K.) 1982, c.11) may contribute to the variability of the experience of widowhood in the future.

Relevant Canadian data are cited wherever possible. Selected data from

U.S. and international studies are utilized as appropriate, especially where Canadian data are limited or lacking. The findings reported derive in large part from two studies of widowhood in which this author has been involved. The first was a pilot study conducted with 26 widows residing in Guelph, Ontario, who were identified through obituary notices appearing in local newspapers. In-depth exploratory interviews were conducted with these women, who ranged in age from 46 to 86 years, widowed an average of 9 years following a marriage lasting an average of 34 years. Findings from this study have been reported elsewhere (Martin Matthews 1982, 1987a, 1987b). Throughout this monograph, this project is referred to as the Guelph pilot study.

The second project studied widowed women and men who were all participants in a panel study conducted by the Gerontology Research Centre at the University of Guelph in 1984 and 1986. The panel consisted of 681 community-dwelling individuals residing in four communities: a rural village, a rural town, a small city, and a metropolitan area. Of these individuals 204 were widowed. Interviews were completed with 152 of them for a response rate of 75 percent. The sample consisted of 24 males and 128 females, with an average age of 75, ranging from 60 through to 90 years. The mean length of widowhood was 10.6 years, although the range was from less than a year through to 54 years of widowhood. This project is referred to as the Ontario widowhood study throughout this monograph.

Each respondent participated in a structured personal interview, averaging one and a half hours in length, which contained a combination of open-ended and forced-choice questions. Throughout this monograph, findings of the quantitative and qualitative data analysis are reported. The quantitative data, including information on demographic characteristics and standardized measures of social support, morale, and kin and friend interaction, contribute to our knowledge of how these widowed individuals compare and contrast with other survey populations.

The qualitative data used throughout this monograph include the responses of widowed individuals to open-ended questions. The verbatim accounts of respondents are frequently relied upon in social science research, because they enable the investigator to capture "the person in his fullness or emptiness" (Daniel Levinson in Sheehy 1976, 21). In the analysis the qualitative data are emphasized. In social science research generally, the use of qualitative data in the course of analysis "fulfils two distinct functions: to illustrate the range of meaning attached to any one category, and to stimulate new insights" (Selltiz et al. 1959, 433).

Inspection of the "raw data" also enables the investigator to develop new and important insights into the topic, a function central to this research.

Much of the analytical effort of social scientists is devoted to establishing relationships between objective characteristics of a group of people and their subjective reactions. However, the demonstration that a relationship exists does not in itself provide an understanding of the way in which the factors are related. The scrutiny of the raw data may be rewarding in the search for such understanding. [Selltiz et al. 1959, 436]

The qualitative data are used not only to give a better understanding of relationships among the quantitative data, but also to help explain when an expected relationship does not exist. They also contribute to the consideration of cases that do not demonstrate the same trends or pattern of relationships as do most of the cases in a study. And further, the analysis of the qualitative data contributes to the elucidation of aspects of phenomena that were not anticipated in the research. The emphasis on the verbatim quotes of the widowed themselves sets this monograph apart from most other studies of the widowed.

CHAPTER 2

BECOMING WIDOWED: THE EXPERIENCE OF AN EXPECTABLE LIFE EVENT

WIDOWHOOD AS A RELATIVE LIFE EVENT

A fundamental characteristic of widowhood is its stress-related nature. There is general consensus in the field of life-event scaling that the death of a spouse is among the most, if not *the* most, stressful of role transitions (Holmes and Rahe 1967; McFarlane et al. 1980). British research found that those who had lost an adult child and a spouse did not regard one as being more painful than the other (Parkes 1986), although there is some debate whether loss of a young child or loss of spouse poses more difficulties for subsequent functioning (Lehman et al. 1987).

Pearlin (1980, 352) found that most "key transitional life events...bring about little or no emotional changes that are sufficiently stable to be discerned." In his research, only one transition raised depression to a higher level than had existed prior to the event: being widowed. Similarly, a study of the impact of role losses upon social support networks found only widowhood to have a negative effect. Widowhood was also the most important predictor of poor health (Wan 1982; 1985).

Evidence of the significant impact of widowhood as a life event also emerged in the Guelph pilot study of the social, emotional, service, and economic supports of widowed women. An assessment of 34 life events was included in the structured interview schedule. These were chosen to represent major events that occur in a person's lifetime and they ranged from things like "when you left home for the first time" to "the birth of a grandchild." After all experienced life events had been sorted into five groups ranging from "did not affect me at all" to "affected me a lot," the widows were asked to rank order, according to impact on their lives, those events that affected them a lot. Without exception, these widows, all a minimum of five and a maximum of ten years into widowhood, indicated that the loss of a spouse had affected them more than any other single life event (Martin Matthews 1982).

In another Ontario study of 450 men and women aged 61 to 70 years, and retired an average of just over three years, the same method for the evaluation of relative life events was used. In that research as well the death of a spouse consistently emerged as the life event that had had the greatest impact on respondents. It ranked first of 34 life events in level of perceived impact. By contrast, retirement ranked 28th of 34 life events, and the end of a marriage through separation or divorce ranked 17th of 34 events (Martin Matthews et al. 1982). These findings are intriguing, for they suggest that the "predictable" and "scheduled" life event of widowhood has a far more significant impact than events not scheduled and predictable in the life course. Given the predictable nature of widowhood and the attendant opportunities for anticipatory socialization, one would not necessarily expect this finding.

Findings from the Ontario widowhood study further illuminate this picture. This research took a somewhat more qualitative approach to the study of widowhood as a relative life event. Widows and widowers were asked to indicate whether, compared to other events that had occurred in their lives, widowhood had affected them quite a lot, a lot, somewhat, or relatively little. Nearly half the sample (45 percent) indicated that it had affected them quite a lot, and an additional 23 percent indicated that widowhood had affected them a lot.

Numerous reasons were given for the perceived high impact of widowhood. Many of the widowed spoke of the loneliness of their lives without a spouse, while others focused on their longing for their spouse as an individual. Their observations suggest that no amount of anticipatory socialization could have prepared them for the intensity of their emotional response to widowhood.

> It affected me quite a lot. I didn't have a perfect marriage, but my husband and I just quietly loved each other so much. I always had to be where he was. He took such care of me...On his retirement I gave everything up to be with him. [Woman aged 78, widowed 1 year]

> It's the loneliness. No one else takes the place of your spouse. There is no one to share with. [Woman aged 74, widowed 7 years]

> Even though I have a great family, I find loneliness hard to bear especially on weekends and holidays. [Woman aged 81, widowed 18 years]

Of course, the experience of widowhood does not necessarily signify the termination of a blissful marriage. One of the prime predictors of the intensity and duration of bereavement is the closeness of the marital relationship (Di Giulio 1989). For some people, the experience of widowhood affected them quite substantially, although not necessarily in a negative way.

> Life changed. It is much quieter now. Since my husband was an alcoholic, life was not always easy before he died. [Woman aged 76, widowed 9 years]

> My life has benefited by my becoming a widow. I had the cruelest husband. [Woman aged 88, widowed 16 years]

Close to 17 percent of the widows and widowers in the Ontario widowhood study indicated that the death of their spouse had affected them relatively little. Indeed, 7 percent indicated that compared with other life events it had affected them very little. These individuals typically focused on the continuity of their lives in widowhood, and how such structural features of their lives as employment outside the home, the ability to drive, and the presence of children helped them to "go on."

In order to further explore the experience of widowhood as a relative life event, these men and women were asked about other life events that had had more of an impact on them than had widowhood. Slightly over a quarter (27 percent) indicated that other life events had affected them more than had widowhood. These included such events as death of a child, marriage, the war, health changes, and the marriage or divorce of a child. In identifying these life events, many of the widowed referred to role transitions that had had a more *negative* impact on them.

> When I lost my daughter....I found that very hard....she was young whereas my husband had had his life. [Woman aged 89, widowed 5 years]

> My second son was separated and my husband never knew...I was prepared for my husband's death; it's natural, but I found my son's divorce is not something you expect, and...it was a terrible blow at the time. [Woman aged 74, widowed 7 years]

A life event having more impact than widowhood need not necessarily be negative, however. Other widowed individuals noted the significance of life events that changed their lives for the better.

> My marriage. Being an only child and under my mother's thumb, getting away from home really changed my life. [Woman aged 67, widowed 1 year]

These findings collectively suggest that while widowhood is typically experienced as a particularly stressful life event, responses to it are still quite variable. In the following section, several factors that contribute to the perceived stressfulness of widowhood are examined. These are the timing of widowhood, forewarning of the spouse's death, the perceived preventability of the death, previous experience of grief and loss, and cultural practices involving grieving.

SOCIALIZATION TO THE ROLE OF WIDOWED PERSON

Through the process of anticipatory socialization, individuals play at roles that one day they will play for real (Himmelfarb and Richardson 1982). The process of anticipatory socialization is particularly important in relation to widowhood because, "as far as the transitional events are concerned, coping does not begin with the emergence of the event, but with its advance anticipation" (Pearlin 1980, 355). The first two factors to be discussed in this section, age at widowhood and forewarning, influence the extent of anticipatory socialization to the role of widowed person.

Age at Widowhood

Like McDaniel's *Canada's Aging Population*, another volume in this Series, Chapter 1 has emphasized how the experience of widowhood has increasingly come to be associated with later life. While women born in the nineteenth century became widows in their late 50s, today widows can expect to be nearly 70 when this life event occurs (Gee 1986). Increasingly, old age is the expected time for widowhood. When events are expected at specific points in the life course, they are perceived in terms of a "social clock" (Neugarten and Hagestad 1976) by which individuals and society assess whether a life event is "on time" or "off time." The expectation of the typical age at widowhood has several implications for how it is experienced by individuals. The experience of widowhood as on time or off time will affect individuals in terms of their psychological preparedness and of opportunities for anticipatory socialization and for the societal resources and supports available to them. Thus, the expectation or anticipation of the death of the spouse may provide the partner with an opportunity to also anticipate what life will be like as a widowed person.

Grief is more intense when death occurs at a young age and when death is relatively unexpected (Vachon et al. 1976; Vachon 1979, 1981). This has been empirically established, especially in relation to depression. Smith (1978) found that, among the recently bereaved, younger widows were more depressed than older ones, but after 18 months there was no significant difference. In a Toronto study of widowers participating in self-help groups, Tudiver et al. (1990, 4) found that, in the early period of bereavement, widowers less than age 65 "were experiencing more psychological and social distress than those 65 and older despite the fact that they had similar social supports."

At early ages, and with unanticipated death, there is typically little opportunity for the anticipatory socialization experienced by older individuals. Patterns of access to a reference group of supportive individuals will also be quite different for members of different age groups. Those widowed in later life usually have access to female siblings and age peers who are themselves already widowed (Balkwell 1985). The issue of age at widowhood and its relationship to long-term adaptation is, however, a complicated one. While Lopata (1979) found that women widowed at younger ages have more personal resources with which to build a new emotionally satisfying network, there is also evidence that the younger the widowed person, the more likely it is that the presence of dependent children will complicate the nature of the transition (Smith 1978). In a 12-year follow-up of German widowed women, those who had been widowed off time gradually experienced improvements in their general well-being largely as a function of "growing into 'normality.'" For these women, "not belonging to a minority group any more...seems to ease the burden and stigma of being a single women in a couple-oriented society" (Fooken 1985, 98).

In contrast, women widowed on time seemed to be "psychologically prepared to accept the death of the spouse as well as their own status of widow" (ibid.). Indeed, Canadian research on widows and widowers an average age of 66, but ranging from age 49 to 83 years, found that "advanced age *per se* may contribute to better adjustment to widowhood" (Haas-Hawkings et al. 1985). The relationship may be curvilinear, however. In comparisons of very old widows (aged 75 and over) and "younger" old widowed (aged 60 to 74), the older group lacked many resources. They had lower incomes, poorer functional health, were less able to drive, were less socially active, and indicated the need for additional instrumental assistance (O'Bryant 1989). While widowhood at a young age is decidedly off time, there are also those for whom widowhood occurs so very late in life that the presence of age-related health decrements and a lack of resources may impede adaptation.

Forewarning of Spouse's Death

While the expectedness of widowhood as a life event varies with age, the duration of the spouse's final illness and forewarning of the death are also factors influencing opportunities for anticipatory socialization to the role of widowed person. A related question is whether the duration of final illness and forewarning allows for anticipatory grieving and better adjustment to widowhood.

There has been considerable debate on this point. *Anticipatory grief* is the term used to describe the grief experienced by an individual upon learning that someone close to him or her is expected to die. There is evidence that individuals who have had opportunity for anticipatory grief do in fact adjust better (Glick et al. 1974; Ball 1977; Vachon, Rogers, et al. 1982; O'Bryant 1991) and exhibit lower levels of depression (Smith 1978). Willis et al. (1987) found that an unexpected event, such as the sudden illness of a loved one, was more stressful than the death of that person if the death was anticipated.

On the other hand, there is also evidence that the duration of the spouse's final illness or forewarning has no relationship to the partner's subsequent adjustment to bereavement (Maddison and Walker 1967; Gerber et al. 1975; Blanchard et al. 1976; Hill et al. 1988; McGloshen and O'Bryant 1988; Roach and Kitson 1989). Indeed, a long final illness, rather than allowing for anticipatory grief and facilitating subsequent adjustment to widowhood, may in fact lead to an outcome directly opposite. Those individuals who cared for their spouses through a long final illness have been found to have adjusted more poorly (Clayton 1973) and to have suffered the consequences of neglecting their own health (Fengler and Goodrich 1979). If anything, the anxiety and stress of the "death watch" may be quite detrimental to the physical and mental health of the survivor. There may in fact be a curvilinear relationship between length of time anticipating the death and survivor morbidity. "Death stings in most cases, but [sudden and unexpected loss of a spouse]... resembles a sharp pain demanding reorganization while [a lengthy time of caring for a spouse] is a dull, chronic pain that delays life reorganization" (Ferraro 1989, 75).

Recent efforts to explain these conflicting research findings suggest that this relationship is mediated by age and by the concept of on-time events as discussed previously. Because widowhood in later life is largely expectable regardless of the specific circumstances of the spouse's death, "even elderly women who lose a spouse suddenly and unexpectedly may actually have, to some extent, anticipated or spontaneously rehearsed for their loss" (Hill et al. 1988, 795). As a result, patterns of adjustment among the elderly widowed for whom the loss was apparently unexpected may in fact be similar to those with more specific warning. There is empirical support for this view. Ball (1977) found that the lack of a relationship between anticipatory grief and bereavement outcome was true among the elderly widowed, but *not* among younger adults. Among younger widows, longer duration of final illness *does* make a difference.

Overall, anticipatory grief does appear to play *some* role in the process of adapting to and coping with widowhood. While certainly the evidence is not conclusive, the widowed who have had forewarning of death generally report higher levels of psychological well-being and adaptation in the 6 to 18 months following the death. Not only does the survivor use the period of forewarning to adapt psychologically; couples may also use this time for "practical planning," such as discussing financial matters (O'Bryant 1991).

Forewarning of the spouse's death may be important to the process of adaptation not only in terms of anticipatory grief and anticipatory social-ization to the role of widowed person, but also in terms of the perception of the death as preventable or not. DiGiulio (1989) reports that even in cases of virtually no forewarning, women whose husbands died in ways that were perceived as more "preventable," such as by suicide, alcohol-related deaths, and some accidents, adapted less well than those whose spouses died in apparently "unpreventable" ways. In a study of individuals bereaved four to seven years previously as a result of a motor vehicle accident, Lehman et al. (1987, 226) found that fully 28 percent of respondents reported thoughts in the previous months of "'If only I had done something different, my spouse would still be alive.'" Over two-thirds (68 percent) felt that they had not been able to find any meaning at all in the death.

Previous Experience of Bereavement and Loss

Researchers have only recently begun to address the issue of whether previous experience of bereavement, or even prior widowhood, facilitates adaptation to a loss. Such a view assumes that the previously bereaved may benefit from coping strategies they developed in the earlier experience. O'Bryant and Straw (1991) did find that recent widows who had experienced the loss of a previous husband appeared somewhat better adapted than widows without such prior experience. The differences were strongest in terms of economic factors and self-sufficient behaviour. Psychological well-being was not enhanced by previous experience of widowhood, however. Indeed, previous widowhood may in fact "contribute to the recent widow's current sense of loss, resulting in a fatalistic attitude and decreased adjustment" (O'Bryant and Straw 1991, 15).

REORGANIZING ONE'S SELF AND WORLD: GRIEF WORK AND COPING

In contrast with North American cultural rituals that typically allow for three days of formal mourning and assume a fairly precipitous return to "normal" functioning, the actual process of bereavement and mourning usually takes considerably longer. Investigations of the processes of "grief work" among the bereaved have found that "not until two years after bereavement did a difference in overall disturbance between intervention and control groups become apparent...The estimate of the duration of adjustment to conjugal bereavement has been steadily extended" (Vachon et al. 1980, 1384). Ferraro and Barresi (1982) found the period of four years after the death of the spouse to be a meaningful demarcation in the process of adjustment and social relations. Nagy (1982) also found the four-year mark a turning point for the widowed. While length of widowhood was not a factor in perceptions of health status among 142 widowed women, those widowed for periods of less than four years reported being "less than happy" more often than those widowed for longer periods of time. Others have argued that "bereavement cannot be assigned a specific amount of time" (DiGiulio 1989, 66).

Whatever the overall length of time required to come to terms with the death of the spouse, the early bereavement period is typically associated with profound psychological disorganization. As the symbolic interactionist perspective recognizes, interaction with significant others provides the basis for the sense of reality of the world, including the way in which one views oneself. Within this framework, what happens when the individual is confronted with the loss of perhaps the "most significant" significant other, the spouse? The Meadian perspective described in Chapter 1 leads us to expect that the widowed individual's sense of self is thrown into jeopardy by the loss of the spouse. The me, the organized set of attitudes of others, will likely be changed by the loss of a primary significant other (the spouse) who has contributed to that definition. Research findings and the autobiographical accounts of widows themselves indicate that this is precisely what happens in bereavement, although to varying degrees depending upon individual circumstances.

> ...It seemed like hours before I could be persuaded to walk out of that room. When I did, I was conscious of my hands dangling uselessly by my sides. I was a person with no job to do, no place to fill, no function in life. The line had been drawn — the line between the world that contained somebody who needed me, and the world that had to go on somehow without him. [Evans 1971, 139]

Berger and Kellner's symbolic interactionist analysis of reality construction in marriage suggests some explanations for why this loss of sense of self may result from the termination of the marital relationship. Every individual requires the ongoing validation of his or her world, especially of identity and place in the world, by truly significant others. For many, the marital relationship becomes the forum in which this validation is primarily achieved, and as a consequence,

> in marriage then, the identity of each now takes on a new character, having to be constantly matched with that of the other, indeed being typically perceived by people at large as being symbolically conjoined with the identity of the other. In each partner's psychological economy of significant others, the marriage partner becomes the other *par excellence*, the nearest and most decisive cohabitant of the world. Indeed all other significant relationships have to be almost automatically reperceived and regrouped in accordance with the drastic shift. [Berger and Kellner 1970, 58]

Such a "drastic shift" having taken place with marriage, the profound changes that will occur in widowhood become apparent. These changes involve nothing short of a complete redefinition on the part of widowed persons of who they are and how they see the world and their place in it. It is a complete alteration of everyday taken-for-granted reality.

Unlike identity changes accompanying marriage, there is evidence that identity changes in widowhood take place at a painfully conscious level. In marriage, the partners may not deliberately set out to re-create their world. The change in identity from single person to spouse, and from defining the world in terms of an "I" perspective to a "we" perspective, "...remains, in bulk, unapprehended and unarticulated" (Berger and Kellner 1970, 63). This process of identity formation has been described as "luckily and necessarily, for the most part unconscious except where inner conditions and outer circumstances combine to aggravate a painful, or elated, *identity consciousness"* (Erikson 1968, 22). One occasion of such identity consciousness is in bereavement, when widowed persons lose the partner with whom they shared the ongoing process of defining not only the world but also themselves.

This experience of identity consciousness may begin immediately upon bereavement. However, the awareness of change may also come about more gradually as widowed people, in going about their everyday worlds, see their behaviours redefined by others, and gradually come to redefine themselves. The widowed may experience a feeling of "stigma,...the change in attitude that takes place in society when a person dies. Every widow discovers that people who were previously friendly and approachable become embarrassed and strained in her presence" (Parkes 1986, 28). Formerly innocent interaction with a friend's husband or a male friend may now be redefined as threatening or as a source of gossip. Clearly, this is a social process, for in terms of the Meadian concept of the self, such reconstruction must characterize widowed persons' definition of themselves. Two factors complicate this process. The first is the perception of widowhood as a devalued status, and the second pertains to norms of appropriate behaviour among the widowed.

There is a general consensus among the widowed that, for women in particular, theirs is a devalued status. Studies indicate that the feeling of being a "second-class citizen" begins the very moment that friends in condolence letters, and in interaction, convey to the widowed just how awkward their loss makes others feel (Caine 1974, 81; Aitken 1975, 5). The lack of a mate in a social network of couples, in a couple-companionate society, contributes to the experience of status loss. However, feelings of status loss may not necessarily be felt by all widowed women and men. This may be particularly true in later life when the fact of being "unattached" is more normative and a large reference group of other widowed persons more readily available. One might also speculate on whether feelings of status loss in widowhood will characterize future cohorts. In a society whose values are more informed by feminist perspectives, the perceived stigma of being unattached may well diminish. A long-term pattern of increasing divorce rates may have a similar effect, although the demographic evidence is clear that at any given point in time the vast majority of Canadians are married or have partners.

The concept of status forcing (Strauss 1959) is relevant to the analysis of perceived status loss in widowhood. This process involves the forcing of individuals, by groups, in and out of all kinds of temporary identities. It is applicable to the study of widowhood in that persons placed in devalued statuses are ritualistically separated from a place in the legitimate order; that is, "[they] must be defined as standing at a place 'outside'; [they] must be made 'strange'" (Strauss 1959, 78).

In the Ontario widowhood study, many individuals referred to their status as that of a "second-class citizen"; or they felt "like a fifth wheel." Fully 53 percent indicated that they had felt this way, with widowers just as likely as widows to report this sentiment. Feeling like an outsider becomes an issue for many widowed people, particularly at social gatherings, although this changes with time. A 77-year-old widow of eight years observed, "At first I certainly felt like a 'fifth wheel' but now I'm getting out more and meeting different ones." Others speculated whether their own attitudes, rather than the attitudes of others, were the source of the problem. A 71-year-old woman widowed one year commented that "I have certainly felt like a second-class citizen.... I'm not sure whether it's just me or... the people I'm with." Such feelings typically subside with time as new non-married friends are acquired, or as married friends themselves become widowed.

Many widowed persons are reluctant to openly admit status loss, but otherwise convey it in their remarks (Lopata 1973b, 90). In a couple-companionate society, being married is a highly sanctioned status, and being widowed is not. Strains in interaction, embarrassment, feeling like a fifth wheel, and being excluded from former activities are all manifestations of a subtle status forcing that renders it very difficult for the widowed to deny a change in others' attitudes towards them, and from this, a change in their own self-image.

Some researchers have referred to widowhood in terms of a "spoiled identity," partly because of the general lack of norms for the appropriate behaviour of the widowed. This lack may leave individuals with quite vague and ambiguous guidelines as they negotiate their new identities and social worlds. Respondents in the Ontario widowhood study frequently observed that "I was amazed how many others expected me to make major changes in my life" (Woman aged 69, widowed 12 years), or noted that "if you pay the least attention to someone else, society misconstrues the situation" (82-year-old man widowed 6 years). The ambiguous, frequently evaluating nature of others' reactions to them made many of the widows in particular feel vulnerable during the initial period of bereavement. The problem of a spoiled identity and the difficulties associated with developing a new identity and sense of self may be particularly trying for the individual who has had few social roles outside the marital relationship or whose employment has been inside the home.

In response to feelings of status loss and a spoiled identity, some widowed persons seek a peer group in which to interact. In such a group widowed persons can replace the lost significant other with generalized others who can empathize with their situation. The seeking of companionship among a reference group of other widowed persons has been more characteristic of widows than of widowers, reflecting the demographic realities noted in Chapter 1. Such groups have been described in the literature as "the society of widows" (Cumming and Henry 1961) or the "merry widows" (Atchley 1972, 298).

In the Meadian perspective, since the incorporation of others' attitudes is necessary for the development of the me, interaction among a group of widowed persons should result in a more positive redefinition of self than that acquired in society at large, where many of the widowed experience a feeling of status loss. Many women in the Ontario widowhood study acknowledged that "most of the people I associate with now are widows" and that "mostly the couples stick together and leave us old widowed ladies alone."

> You see someone else with a partner and you know yours is gone. You feel alone, on the outside. If you are with other widows, you don't feel so out of place. [Woman aged 65, widowed 3 years]

Despite the initial psychological disruption of bereavement, many individuals experience widowhood as an opportunity for growth and independence. One qualitative study of older single women found that, for some women, the death of the spouse in later life gave them "their first independent feeling of 'this is my life now'" (Allen 1989, 19). For these women, independence was a "process of gaining selfhood," expressed either behaviourally or in more psychological terms, reflecting a sense of becoming "different" (ibid.). Fully 57 percent of the widowed in the Ontario study felt that being widowed had changed them personally. Most reported that they were now more independent, more thoughtful and appreciative, more decisive, and that they had "mellowed." These findings are consistent with other research which shows that approximately half of the widowed feel freer and more independent than they did before widowhood (Lopata 1973b, 88), particularly in terms of independence of time and decision making (Harvey and Bahr 1974) and freedom from family responsibilities (Allen 1989).

Using surveys of 223 members of mutual self-help organizations for the widowed, Silverman (1987) developed a typology of problematic accommodation to widowhood (remaining psychologically committed to the past) versus satisfactory adjustment (changing the way one relates to oneself or others and feeling satisfied with one's life). She noted that many widowed women "moved to positions of autonomy," deriving satisfaction from their newly acquired skills in decision making and managing their lives. Among widowers, change resulted in "bringing them closer to the way women saw themselves when they married," exhibiting more "mutuality" and caring than existed before (Silverman 1987, 189). Overall she concluded that "in studying outcome [of widowhood] we cannot talk about recovery but of transformation" (1987, 189). This transformation may in fact be central to successful adaptation, for "adjustment to widowhood without a movement *beyond* it can be a 'life sentence' for the widow" (DiGiulio 1989, 89).

There is evidence of such transformation in the accounts of participants in the Ontario widowhood study.

> I've blossomed out into my own personality. When I married I got into my husband's ways. I wear different types of clothes now. I can be me. I used to be jealous of the garden and music; they got more of my husband's attention than I did. [Woman aged 67, widowed 1 year]

> I became more independent, a lot more my own person. You have to, to be on your own without your husband's help.... It makes you a stronger person. You have to make your own decisions. [Woman aged 83, widowed 14 years]

> I never thought I'd be able to cope. It makes you stronger. My family and friends thought I coped very well... When you're put to the test, it's surprising what you can do. [Woman aged 85, widowed 16 years]

For others, however, the changes brought with widowhood were perceived as more negative. These individuals spoke of "feeling lost," "feeling helpless...and very vulnerable," of feeling that "widowhood has made my life a lot smaller."

> I don't have a sense of belonging now. What I did throughout my life was tied with his work... Also, he was on home dialysis for six years and I assisted him with this, and this was my life. [Woman aged 63, widowed 2 years] [1]

Although widowers are somewhat more likely than widows to perceive changes in themselves as negative, most widowed people do in time feel that they have been strengthened by this life transition and that it has evoked a realization of their own strength.

These findings lend support to Berger and Kellner's observation that the sharing of future horizons in marriage inevitably involves a narrowing of the future projections of each partner. "Having now considerably stabilized his self image, the married individual will have to project the future in accordance with this maritally defined identity" (Berger and Kellner 1970, 63). With widowhood, the struggle to resolve the identity crisis is so acutely conscious that not only do the widowed arrive at more positive self-definitions, but they are also able to develop a separate, independent identity, without the help of their "most" significant other (Lopata 1973b, 412).

In the words of one widow,

> I don't exactly remember the date when I stopped introducing myself as "___, Widow"; nor do I remember marking down the day I took off my wedding band... There have been so many ups and downs...and gradually learning that there's a whole ME, a separate being, apart from any HE. I've struggled and fought damn hard for my sanity and independence. [Seskin 1975, 168]

> I am not quite the vulnerable quivering oyster that I was...You are slowly fading and I know that's how it's meant to be [Robson 1974, 217, 221; account of a widow's letters to her dead husband]

The process of social and psychological adaptation to widowhood follows no particular pattern or sequence of stages, however. For most widowed people, two years marks a transition point when they have by and large completed the process of grief work. But reactions can occur for years after the death, and the needs of the recently and long-term widowed may be surprisingly parallel. In the words of clinicians, "We give time too much credit as a healer" (Barrett and Schneweis 1980-1981, 102). The following sections of this chapter examine health-related outcomes among the widowed, and selected coping strategies utilized in the process of adaptation.

MORBIDITY AND MORTALITY AMONG THE RECENTLY BEREAVED

Considerable attention has been paid to the issue of how life events, either desirable or undesirable, affect the health of the individual who has experienced the transition. Because of the stressful nature of widowhood, as discussed earlier in this chapter, the assumption has been that widowhood has a strong negative effect on the health status of the bereaved. Research on this topic has taken several forms: studies of the younger widowed, focusing in particular on the relationship between widowhood and mortality; more recent investigations of the immediate and longer-term impact of bereavement on illness episodes, referred to as morbidity; and studies of the relationship between widowhood and mental health. Each of these is examined in this discussion.

Research findings to date on the relationship between morbidity and widowhood have been somewhat equivocal. There is some evidence that the health status of the elderly is largely unaffected by widowhood (Heyman and Gianturco 1973), but other evidence indicates health decrements following the loss of a spouse (Fenwick and Barresi 1981). The contradictory nature of these research findings can largely be attributed to the fact that health and illness are multidimensional concepts, including not only subjective and objective evaluations of health status but also health behaviours, health beliefs, and such health attitudes as optimism or pessimism (Chappell et al. 1986). This point is well recognized in research by Ferraro, who found that while widowhood results in an immediate decrease in perceived health among older people, it has minimal long-term impact. Widowhood also did not diminish the health optimism of individuals, and, indeed, health optimism increased among widows aged 75 and over. This suggests that "people contextualize their evaluation of health, and the expectations accompanying sex and age are far more important than marital status in the process of constructing health perceptions" (Ferraro 1985-1986, 20).

There is no consensus on the relationship between widowhood and mortality (Kestenbaum and Diez 1982). Research has focused on two related questions. The first is whether mortality rates are higher for bereaved than for non-bereaved persons of comparable age, and the second is whether observed mortality rates among the bereaved decrease with the passage of time since the loss of the spouse. Despite highly publicized clinical studies in England that document unexpectedly high mortality rates among widowers in the first six months following the death of their wives (Young et al. 1963; Parkes 1970), epidemiological studies have generally failed to corroborate these findings (Helsing and Szklo 1981; Kestenbaum and Diez 1982).

Studies of the relationship between mental health and widowhood typically focus on the issue of coping styles and abilities. The early period of bereavement is generally acknowledged to be associated with depression, mood alterations, disrupted sleep patterns, obsessive thoughts or even hallucinations about the deceased, and disorientation (Balkwell 1981; Sawa 1986). However, only about one in five widowed persons manifests significant difficulty in coping with the spouse's death two years after bereavement (Lund et al. 1985-1986). A comparison of widowed persons and a control group of non-widowed persons in a national U.S. study found that the widowed took "approximately one decade to approach control respondent's scores on life satisfaction, and over two decades to approach their scores on depression" (Wortman and Silver 1990, 251). Rates of both institutional and non-institutional psychiatric treatment are higher among the widowed than among comparable married individuals (Robertson 1974), and rates of suicide are higher as well (Rico-Velasco and Mynko 1973). All of these rates are higher for younger than for older widowed individuals. Typically, the widowed with dependent children have the worst short-term outcomes in terms of depressive symptoms and adjustment problems.

Long-term outcomes are more difficult to determine. Recent research suggests that age, for example, is not an important factor in the morale of widowed persons and that to be widowed early in life does not lead to deleterious long-term consequences for morale (Balkwell 1985). On the other hand, an analysis of data from the Canada Health Survey on individuals over age 40 suggests that widowed persons are less happy and more negative in mood than are the non-widowed, although this difference is only significant among lower socio-economic groups. However, the impact of widowhood on morale was similar for all age groups (Harvey et al. 1987).

Complex relationships exist, however, between mental health, morbidity, and mortality. Among the widowed, health has been found to have a significant impact on psychological well-being (McGloshen and O'Bryant 1988). Conversely, psychological distress following bereavement may be associated with behaviours that increase the risk of morbidity and mortality. Behaviours that reflect "avoidant coping strategies" include the use of alcohol or tranquillizers, changes in eating behaviour, increases in sleep, and the avoidance of people. Although used infrequently by the widowed, these strategies are associated with high levels of distress at 12 months following bereavement (Gallagher et al. 1989). Their use declines by 30 months after the death of the spouse. Other research has found evidence of an increased use of alcohol in response to bereavement. A Harvard University study examining predictors of poor outcome among 68 younger widows and widowers found evidence at six weeks of "drinking more alcohol than before bereavement" (Parkes 1986). A Canadian study of alcoholism among the elderly profiled two types of "reactive drinkers." Some were long-term drinkers who, in response to bereavement, heavily increased their consumption of alcohol; others, representing "lifetime 'normal social drinkers' ...whose drinking became problematic in response to grief...did appear in the cases studies, but only rarely" (Graham et al. 1989, 11). Evidence of this pattern also emerged in the Ontario widowhood study. Conversely, however, widowhood may serve to facilitate a successful outcome of a problem with alcohol. Graham et al. (1989) found that alcohol consumption actually dropped for some elderly persons for whom the death of the spouse ended worry and anxiety associated with the spouse's deteriorating health.

Overall, these data suggest that many psychological and physical changes are associated with the transition from married to widowed person. Subsequent chapters examine the utilization of social and personal resources in coping with the transitions associated with widowhood. Among some widowed persons, however, remarriage is an alternative response to the death of their spouse.

REMARRIAGE AS A COPING RESPONSE

Among the widowed, remarriage is an option selected by only a few (Connidis 1989b). As indicated in Chapter 1, remarriage following widowhood is far more characteristic of widowers than of widows, although rates for both are quite low overall. In fact, rates of remarriage among the widowed have actually declined in recent years. Census data indicate that in 1971 one in four widowers would eventually remarry. In the 1980s, by contrast, less than one in five widowers could expect to remarry. Among widows, the drop in the rate of remarriage has been even more precipitous. While in 1971 approximately 1 in 10 widows remarried, this figure had dropped to 1 in 20 by 1984. In sum, the likelihood of remarriage for widows and widowers has declined by over 40 percent (Statistics Canada 1988). Not only are rates of remarriage low (see also the discussion in Chapter 1), but also the widowed who do remarry are on the average considerably younger than the widowed population as a whole. The average age at remarriage for widowers is 64 years; for widows it is 58 years (Statistics Canada 1988).

The apparent reticence of the widowed in opting for remarriage as a coping response to the loss of a spouse is not well understood, although age at the time of the spouse's death is an important factor. The older the widowed person, the lower the probability of remarriage. Strength of interest in remarriage is inversely age-related, being less frequently expressed by older than by younger women (Rosenman and Shulman 1987). In this context, the apparent effects of age could be masking other important considerations, such as age-related health and financial concerns, cohort-specific attitudes towards marriage, or societal views of the appropriateness of marriage and sexuality in later life (Gentry and Shulman 1988). DiGiulio notes a societal discouragement of remarriage among the elderly, "a vague 'unseemliness' about remarriage — and new relationships — among widowed people" (1989, 130). More pragmatically, widows may reject remarriage because of the fear of an elderly new husband getting sick and requiring an indefinite or burdensome period of care (Allen 1989). Another constraining factor may be the process of "sanctification of the spouse's memory," as described by Lopata (1981). This refers to a process whereby widows have been found to idealize their deceased spouse and to consider him "an unusually good man" whose attributes could not be found in another person. Loyalty to the deceased spouse may also serve as a deterrent to remarriage. A British study of 22 widows found that "many of the widows still seemed to regard themselves as married to their dead husband and remarriage would have been a form of infidelity" (Parkes 1986, 117).

Relatively little is known about the social or psychological aspects of remarriage decisions following widowhood (Gentry and Shulman 1988). Stryckman's research in Quebec is one of the few Canadian studies to focus on the process of becoming remarried following the death of the spouse. She observed that the experience of widowhood as a painful life event was associated with a decreased desire to remarry for the women, and an increased desire to remarry for the men. The widows had been more actively involved in, and thus were more exhausted by, the experience of a long period of care for an ill spouse. Widowers, on the other hand, had tended to rely on other women to help when their wives were terminally ill. It was also apparent that relations with children constituted the single biggest obstacle for those who wished to remarry, particularly for those who strongly identified themselves as mothers (Stryckman 1982, 75).

Even for those who desire it, however, remarriage is not a viable option for many, especially widows. In reflecting the demographic reality as described in Chapter 1, one widow noted, "I hate being a glut on the market" (Robson 1974, 216). Among the respondents in the Ontario widowhood study, the possibility of remarriage was alluded to by only a few, most particularly by the widowers.

> My wife encouraged me to remarry. She picked out some possible wives for me. But she was special, so no one could compare. [Man aged 73, widowed 20 years]

While the greater availability of a potential spouse may make remarriage a more viable option for widowers than for widows, Gentry and Shulman also suggest that "marriage may benefit men more than it does women" (1988, 192). Remarriage is associated with lower mortality rates for widowers than for widows, and may well be a more attractive coping response for widowers because of the greater contribution of marriage to their overall well-being.

Close personal friendships with members of the opposite sex are also relatively uncommon among the widowed. One study of non-married elderly women found that they generally assume that a cross-sex friendship includes romance or courtship (Adams 1985). Only 6 percent of the widows in a Chicago study had remarried, and less than a quarter had developed close personal ties with another man since widowhood (Lopata 1979). Recent research shows that widowers are more willing than widows to establish close cross-sex friendships, and hence are more willing to consider the possibility of remarriage. In research at Sunnybrook Medical Centre in Toronto, Tudiver et al. (1990) found that among a sample of 113 men, widowed an average of 5.5 months, almost 11 percent were already involved in a new "romantic" relationship. Parkes (1986, 230) found significant gender differences in willingness to consider remarriage by the third month following bereavement.

Gentry and Shulman (1988) examined the relation between widowed individuals' consideration of remarriage and their perceptions of emotional distress and their concerns or needs. They postulated that widows should be more likely to consider remarriage or to remarry under conditions of greater distress or more needs, or both. Controlling for age, they found that remarried widows did indeed report the fewest current concerns. However, there was no relationship between considerations of remarriage and perceptions of current distress. A possible explanation for this finding is that remarriage following widowhood may generate its own stresses, resulting in an overall level of distress similar to that of the widowed.

CONCLUSION

As a relative life event, widowhood is considered among the most stressful of role transitions. Although research findings are somewhat equivocal, there is evidence that the timing of widowhood in the life course and the duration of the spouse's final illness contribute significantly to difficulties in adaptation during the bereavement period. The experience of widowhood as on time or off time affects individuals in terms of their psychological preparedness, their opportunities for anticipatory socialization, and the societal resources and supports available to them. Similarly, the duration of the spouse's final illness also influences opportunities for anticipatory socialization to the role of widowed person. However, this relationship appears to be stronger in the case of early, off-time widowhood than for widowhood in later life.

Estimates of the duration of time for the completion of grief work among the bereaved suggest a period of two to four years for adjustment to the loss of the spouse. While the early bereavement period is typically associated with profound psychological disorganization and feelings of status loss, widowhood also provides opportunities for personal growth and independence.

Research on the relationship between widowhood and morbidity and mortality is fraught with contradictory findings. While there is evidence of short-term decreases in health status and perceived health following widowhood, long-term health appears largely unaffected. Despite early research findings of high mortality rates among widowers, more current epidemiological studies have found no significant relationship between bereavement and mortality. Findings of the long-term impact of widowhood on mental health are similarly equivocal, although the early bereavement period is generally associated with depression, mood alterations, disrupted sleep patterns, obsessive thoughts of the deceased, and disorientation.

While remarriage is one form of coping response available to the widowed, census data indicate that less than 1 in 5 widowers and 1 in 20 widows do eventually remarry. In the next chapter, the focus shifts from the social, psychological, and physical responses of individuals to bereavement to a consideration of the broader social contexts within which the widowed negotiate a new identity and social world.

NOTES

1.   This comment well illustrates the point that "the 'normal' period of family life that was disrupted by the death may thus have been one of constant care for an ill patient, rather than one of full family functioning" (Lopata 1975, 218).

CHAPTER 3

BEING WIDOWED: SOCIAL SUPPORTS AND SOCIAL NETWORKS

INTRODUCTION

In order to understand more fully the context of life course transitions such as widowhood, and the meanings that such events have in the lives of those experiencing them, one cannot just focus on individuals in isolation. We each live in a world of significant others and travel through the life course with both ongoing and successive groups of them. The dynamics of these relationships shape our experience of life course transitions, but they are rarely considered in depth in research. The nature of these links between the widowed individual and the larger society is the focus of this chapter. These ties are frequently conceptualized and measured in terms of social support, although, as will be discussed later, this characterization may not be entirely accurate. Lopata's pioneering work on this topic (1979) was based on a definition of the support system as "that set of personal contacts through which the individual maintains social identity and style of life." Widowhood generally disorganizes previous patterns of support and often necessitates the modification of old social relationships and roles (Harvey and Bahr 1984; Lopata 1973b; Martin Matthews 1982). The process and the nature of these modifications are the subject of this chapter.

One conclusion of Lopata's (1979) research on the social supports of metropolitan widows was that the complexity of the support network varies considerably. In her research some of the widowed (all of whom were women in her study) had virtually no contributors to their support network; others relied on a few people for most of their support; and others maintained complex networks with different people who contributed to different supports. In developing an understanding of such variability, this chapter examines the extent to which patterns of support vary in terms of the characteristics of those involved in the support networks of the widowed: aged parents, siblings, children, other kin, friends, and neighbours.

THE CONCEPTUALIZATION AND MEASUREMENT OF SOCIAL SUPPORT

The role and function of social support in the lives of the aged has been extensively examined within the field of social gerontology. A number of studies (Bowling and Cartwright 1982; Lopata 1979; Wan 1982) have examined the effect of a particular age-related stressful life event on several dimensions of physical and mental health, and the role of social support as a mediator or buffer in this relationship. The role of social support becomes an integral component of such analyses because of the perception of its "generally salutary but unspecifiable effect on health" (Bloom as cited in Gottlieb 1981, 28).

There now exists ample evidence that social support plays an important role in the maintenance of health and also in reducing susceptibility to illness in older persons (Cobb 1976; Kaplan et al. 1977; Kulys and Tobin 1980; Pilisuk and Minkler 1980). In examining the important health-promoting functions of support network members, many studies have focused specifically on the family as "one crucial form of social support" (Bohm and Rodin 1985, 280), particularly in relation to such age-related life events as retirement and bereavement.

However, the exact role played by social support in mediating the effect of stressful life events in old age is increasingly acknowledged to be quite complex and, for a variety of reasons, is not well understood. Gottlieb, for example, notes that

> The nature, meaning, and measurement of the social support construct itself are still being intensely debated in the literature...and this lack of agreement about operational and conceptual definitions contributes to our present inability to compare and summarize studies that investigate the empirical effects of social support on health. [1981, 31]

Research on the role of social support in the transition to widowhood has attempted to delineate precisely who participates in the support network of the widowed, and whether their support makes any difference. Researchers have also attempted to clarify further the functions of members of the social support network of the widowed, by focusing on the relative importance of particular sources of support as widowed persons move from the early adjustment phase to a point where their grief is lessened enough to allow them to begin a new life. A study of 51 older Toronto residents widowed 4 to 12 weeks hypothesized that a stable, intimate, and active social network was related to the bereaved person's immediate psychosocial adjustment. That this hypothesis was not supported may suggest that mobilization of the social network as a resource becomes important at a later stage in bereavement (Haas-Hawkings et al. 1985).

Research on social support in widowhood has also questioned the assumption that the widowed person's need for support is fixed and, therefore, that types and sources of support beneficial during one phase of bereavement are equally beneficial at a different phase. Bankoff (1983a; 1983b) examined the function of different supports by source (parent, child, neighbour) and by type (attention, intimacy) for women in two phases: the crisis phase of less than 18 months after bereavement, when all the widows said they were still in the midst of intense grief, and the transition phase, 19 to 36 months after bereavement, when the widows reported that they were still grieving, but to a limited extent. The relative importance of sources of support was a function of the phase of widowhood.

During the crisis phase, parents, followed by widowed or single friends, were the most salient sources of support, reflecting the important nurturing function that an older parent can provide, particularly considering that, for Bankoff's middle-aged widows, "parent" typically meant a mother who had herself experienced widowhood.

During the transition phase, Bankoff found that the salient supports shifted to include, in rank order, widowed or single friends, neighbours, parents, and children. The maintenance of social contact with married friends was, if anything, negatively associated with adjustment to bereavement during this stage. Bankoff suggests that the widening of the network of salient supports reflects the fact that the widowed person at this stage manifests less need for nurturance and more need for information and new social contacts to help reintegrate her life as a single person. She concludes that "the role of social support for women suffering conjugal bereavement is important but complex. Whether support helps, hurts, or is inconsequential for the psychological well-being of widows during their lengthy process of adjustment seems to depend upon at least three factors: where the widow is in the adjustment process; the specific type of support provided; and the source of that support" (Bankoff 1983b, 837).

In the context of this overview of the role of social support in widowhood, it is also necessary to consider another complicating feature of the study of supports to the elderly widowed: the assumption of the inherent value of social support. "The implicit assumption operating in the literature has been that the more support the widow receives (and this usually has meant the more contact she has with family members), the better off she is bound to be. This inference of effectiveness from quantity is highly questionable" (Bankoff 1983b, 828).

Indeed, some Canadian research suggests that a loose rather than a tight supportive network, particularly of family ties, may be a disadvantage in the initial period of bereavement, but may in fact facilitate the reorganization of social roles later in widowhood. Building upon Granovetter's concept of the "strength of weak ties," Walker et al. suggest that "a closely knit network made up predominantly of relatives could become a disadvantage to the widow if she seeks to make new friends, find a job, or develop a new life style" (1977, 39). They maintain that while such networks are appropriate for maintaining a static social identity, in widowhood a woman's identity "is anything but static." High-density networks are in fact often associated with greater symptomatology, poorer mood, and lower self esteem. By contrast, low-density networks comprising individuals not necessarily known to each other and without reciprocal relationships may enable the widowed "to develop new social roles consonant with their changed status" (Vachon and Stylianos 1988, 177).

While most research on social support "assumes the supportive nature of social relationships while neglecting important negative aspects" (Chappell and Guse 1989, 222), other research acknowledges that we have overemphasized the role of social support in ameliorating stressful life events and overemphasized the role of the family in providing primary support. Gottlieb, for example, decries the fact that "family" is virtually assumed to be a part of the social support network, and yet "one need not be a clinician to recognize that family members and friends do not always merit the appellation 'support system', and the fact that this sort of labelling is widespread in the literature reveals something about the romanticism or myopia that has seeped into research on the topic of social support" (1981, 30). There is evidence that contact with family members does little to elevate morale among the widowed aged (Arling 1976), and that while support may promote feelings of independence, "there is a threshold point beyond which continued support may lead to dependence" (Chappell and Guse 1989, 222).

The presence of social support may in fact be associated with negative outcome among the widowed. Focus group interviews with 41 participants in widow support groups found that the widows more often referred to family in a negative than in a positive manner, and concluded that networks "may actually hinder coping" (Morgan 1989, 103). This was especially true when others were perceived as encouraging the belief that grief had been resolved, although the widowed themselves were not yet ready to entertain notions of a return to normalcy. Another U.S. study of widows and widowers, with an average age of 65, and interviewed at six weeks, and 6, 12, 18, and 24 months following bereavement, found that higher levels of social support were consistently associated with higher levels of perceived stress (O'Brien 1987). This was true even for those who showed considerable stability in their social networks over time. O'Brien concluded that the "disruption of marital ties so drastically erodes the effectiveness of close ties in providing social support that considerable time is necessary to reassemble the support system" (1987, 54).

An alternative explanation is offered by Greene and Feld, who similarly found that active involvement in social supports was associated with the presence of negative affect and unhappiness among widows, but not among married women. Support may be given to widowed persons, particularly the recently widowed, because of the problems they manifest and the level of distress they are experiencing. As a consequence, widowed persons with the greatest levels of distress may in fact receive more support than those exhibiting less distress, leading to a positive relationship between levels of distress and social support (Greene and Feld 1989).

The issue of the provision of social support in relation to later-life widowhood is clearly a complex one. This is apparently a case where one can have too much of a good thing. Research findings suggest that the potential benefits of support will be offset if there is too much support, if it comes at the wrong time in the process of adaptation, if it is too intensely focused upon the widowed, or if it is offered only by those with one particular set of attributes.

In spite of all these limitations, the provision and receipt of social support appears to work well in the lives of most elderly widowed persons. The lack of it is clearly problematic. In an analysis of 81 widows aged 55 to 69 who were participants in a longitudinal study of social support in widowhood, a perceived lack of social support accounted for fully 25 percent of the variance in distress levels 1 month after bereavement. In follow-up interviews it accounted for 12 and 13 percent at 6 and 12 months respectively, and only at 24 months did it decrease to 5 percent (Vachon 1981). Many studies highlight the central importance of social support in the lives of individuals after widowhood. Overall, it appears that potential supporters serve three major functions in the lives of the recently bereaved: to smooth the transition to the role of widowed person; to offer support and guidance as the widowed individual seeks to establish a new identity that may or may not reflect the expectations of others; to reject or ignore the widowed, resulting in a lonely isolated life or providing an incentive to develop new relationships (Vachon 1981). Members of the social support networks of the widowed are typically diverse, although most research has focused primarily on the role of children. The following section examines the support patterns and functions of both kin and non-kin members of the support networks of the widowed.

For the purposes of this discussion, a distinction is made between formal and informal supports. Three specific types of tasks have been identified that "primary groups such as families are more structurally effective in handling than bureaucracies" (Shanas and Sussman 1977, 5). These tasks include looking after one's own or another person's physical needs, socio-emotional issues best addressed by primary or reference groups, and tasks concerned with idiosyncratic events (Shanas and Sussman 1977). Thus, informal supports may encompass a broad range of activities involving social support, emotional support, and provision of services.

Formal support structures, on the other hand, typically involve bureaucratic structures "organized to handle uniform tasks using an ever-developing technology, vast resources, and extension lines of communication, buttressed by the ideology of merit and the model of rationality" (Shanas and Sussman 1977, 6). Formal supports include those accessed through government agencies, purchased services, and other kinds of organizations.

THE ROLE OF CHILDREN

Adult children are usually considered to be the linchpin of the informal support network. Most older people, and most of the widowed, have children. While about 80 percent of older people have at least one child, Canadian research has found that about 20 percent of the aged have only one child, "pointing to some structural fragility in this social support resource" (Rosenthal 1987, 315). Even where children exist, factors like geographical mobility and competing role demands on adult children may preclude their active involvement as functional supports in the life of their widowed parent. For example, despite the fact that rural families are typically large, the consequences of the high geographical mobility of young adults are such that, according to one study, only one-fifth of rural elderly respondents had children in the same township (Cape 1987).

In terms of adult children as sources of support, patterns vary among different types of widows. Canadian research has found that what might be described as the "traditional" widow role is usually assumed by older working-class women, or those from a more traditional ethnic background. These women typically move after widowhood to be closer to their adult children, who are sources of practical assistance. Their social networks mostly comprise both children and other widows and "unattached" women. A primary focus of the support of adult children is getting their mothers into new activities; adult children also work hard to encourage their mothers to maintain old contacts as potential sources of remarriage or employment (Vachon 1981).

There is substantial evidence that adult children provide most of the care received by older, widowed parents (Connidis 1989b; Lopata 1979). It appears that emotionally close relationships that are also based on obligation, such as those with children, are not substantially changed by the widowhood of the parent (Anderson 1984, 113). If anything, the widowed have greater contact with their children than do married elders. Data from the Ontario widowhood study confirm the active role of children as functionally involved in supportive relationships with their widowed parents. As will be discussed further in Chapter 4, frequency of contact is higher with children than with any other type of supporter, including siblings, other relatives, and friends. This pattern is consistent for both face-to-face and telephone contact. In addition, children are among the preferred sources of support in situations where the elderly require advice, tangible assistance, or socio-emotional support (Tables 4.2 and 4.4). Similarly, in a Manitoba study of 141 middle-aged widows, Harris and Harvey (1987) found that 68 percent of the widows had daily contact with their children, and that, overall, children were the most significant sources of support to widows in the processes of decision making. The literature on relations between the widowed parent and the adult child generally suggests that "age, gender and marital status interact, leading to more frequent contact with children among older, widowed women than among other subgroups" (Rosenthal 1987, 319). The particular circumstances of widowers in their relationship to children are discussed further in Chapter 4.

High levels of contact between the widowed and their adult children are, however, not necessarily uniform, either across children or in terms of the duration of widowhood. As discussed by Connidis (1989b) in *Family Ties and Aging*, another volume in this Series, daughters figure prominently as sources of support to the aged. Lopata (1979, 203) describes daughters as "unquestionably the people the widow feels closest to. She enjoys them and they make her feel important." This has been empirically established in the Canadian context as well (Rosenthal 1987; Stone 1988). Australian data similarly suggest that daughters have more diffuse and stronger ties with their mothers (McCallum 1986). While in some cases this is an extension of a lifelong relationship, many daughters report that their influence over their mother's life and decision making increased with the mother's widowhood and advancing age (Pratt et al. 1989).

This is not to say that sons do not play a role in the social support networks of a widowed parent. Horowitz (1985) found that sons provide almost as much emotional support, financial assistance, and assistance in accessing services as daughters, but that they are less likely than daughters to help with instrumental or hands-on services.

There is also evidence that high levels of support from adult children are more specific to the earlier, post-bereavement stages of widowhood and that such support decreases with time. Vachon and Stylianos (1988) found that, while the support of adult children is crucial during the periods of acute grief which typify the initial period of bereavement, it becomes less important over time as new and previous friends increase in importance.

An issue related to the receipt of support from adult children involves the perceived impact of this support on the lives of the widowed. Most widowed people in the Ontario study expressed satisfaction with the amount of contact with their children. "We get along beautifully. We couldn't have a better relationship" (Woman aged 74, widowed 12 years). Others looked to children to help "fill in the gap" when they were feeling bereft or felt a lack.

I would like to see and hear more from them all. Being alone without a husband, I am lonesome. [Woman aged 74, widowed 8 years]

It would be so nice to see her more often because she's all I've got. [Woman aged 78, widowed 1 year]

Other widowed persons felt restricted by the presence of adult children. "Sometimes when you think you might have some quiet he's there disturbing you" (Woman aged 85, widowed 21 years). For some, the desire to reduce contact was born not of dissatisfaction with the relationship, but of a sense that too frequent contact might undermine it.

My daughter would like more contact. However, there is an art to being a father-in-law. My daughter and her husband need time together in order to make their relationship flourish. Therefore I refuse most of their invitations. [Man aged 67, widowed 3 years]

However, relations between the widowed and their adult children can exhibit quite complex and even contradictory patterns. In a Quebec study, the frequency of interaction with children was found to decrease over time in widowhood, but the widowed felt quite positively about this change (Stryckman 1982). This may well reflect, as Bankoff (1983a; 1983b; 1986) notes, changes over time in the widowed's need for nurturance, and a move to increased independence and resiliency. Even in those cases where adult children worry a great deal about their widowed parents and are generally considered attentive, there may be avoidance of discussions concerning the widowed parent's feelings, circumstances, and prospects. In a survey of middle-aged children in Hamilton, Synge (1988) found that there was little discussion between adult children and their parent(s) of issues related to widowhood or the possibility of dependency in late life. The event most likely to precipitate such conversations was the widowed parent's own illness.

Another factor potentially influencing the pattern of relationships between the widowed and their adult children concerns the marital status of the adult children themselves. A study of middle-aged widowed women found that elderly "parents are the single most important source of support gained from the informal support network; parental support is related most strongly to the psychological well-being of these recently widowed women" (Bankoff 1983a, 229). In that study, "parents" typically meant mother, a women of about age 75 who was herself widowed. This is a special case of relations between a widowed elderly woman and an adult child where the child and her mother share the same role of widow, thus making "social age peers of persons who are not chronological age peers" (Hagestad 1981, 17). Indeed, Hagestad argues that unless unforeseen demographic patterns intervene, families will increasingly experience a pattern of two generations of retirees, "followed by a stage with two generations of widows" (Hagestad 1981, 23).

Research findings suggest that aged parents may play a quite significant and unique role in the lives of their adult children. In relation to the study of widowhood in later life, these findings encourage the recognition that not only are the elderly widowed recipients of support from adult children and involved in reciprocal exchanges with them, but they also may provide significant support to others under particular circumstances. Even in cases where an adult child is not herself widowed, support from a widowed parent is not atypical. Nor is this support restricted to social and emotional assistance. Analyses of patterns of intergenerational economic support in the U.S. Longitudinal Retirement History panel show that assistance from older parents to younger generations frequently continues even as parents experience major age-related role transitions. Widowed parents were no more likely than the non-widowed to reduce economic support to children, nor were widows less likely to continue financially assisting children than were widowers (Morgan 1983).

Adult children clearly play a significant role in the support systems of their widowed parent. Although some researchers, as noted earlier in this chapter, have found that contact with adult children is not associated with elderly parents' levels of well-being, Morgan (1976) did find that higher levels of family interaction were in fact associated with higher morale for both married and widowed persons. However, much of the gerontological literature that examines the family relations of the widowed focuses almost exclusively on the parent-child relationship. Other family ties are also of importance to the aged. Predominant among these is the tie between the widowed and their siblings.

THE ROLE OF SIBLINGS

Sibling bonds are unique among one's intimate relationships in terms of their longer duration in comparison with other family ties and their essentially egalitarian nature (Connidis 1989b, 71). Generally the research literature indicates quite strong patterns of emotional support between the aged and their siblings, although patterns of contact and exchange of assistance and tangible support may be quite low. Studies have found that widowhood unites siblings, bringing emotional closeness between the bereaved and their brothers and sisters (Ross and Milgram 1982; Anderson 1984, 1987). This point of view was consistently reiterated by participants in the Ontario widowhood study.

> We go out together frequently. We make quilts together in winter. We share news of family. We're quite 'open' with each other. My sisters and I can talk about anything. I'm lucky to have two sisters. We've always been close. [Woman aged 72, widowed 3 years]

> I think you should keep in touch with family....I enjoy talking with my sister. We can talk about people and experiences in the past that I can't talk about with anyone else. [Male aged 79, widowed 4 years]

There is evidence, however, that sibling ties may change with time, sometimes becoming closer and other times less close. In the Ontario study, 31 percent indicated that their relationships with their siblings had changed.

> As we got older our children were grown and we didn't have the same interests. As the others started to pass away our ties became less close. [Woman aged 91, widowed 10 years]

> I'm closer to them now that we are older. When we were young there was such an age difference, but now it doesn't matter. [Woman aged 68, widowed 15 years]

The shared experience of the transition to widowhood itself may strengthen sibling ties as well. As one person observed, "We've always been close, but have grown closer since we lost our husbands" (Woman aged 80, widowed 12 years). For others, the closeness has always been there. "We've always been a good family, not really close like we cling but caring for each other and watching out for each other" (Woman aged 72, widowed 4 years).

In the few cases where acrimony rather than affection appeared to characterize the ties between the widowed and their siblings, it was striking how frequently issues of religion, education, and finances were cited as divisive forces.

> I have essentially no contact with my sister...I used to feel close to her. She thinks she's superior due to her education. [Man aged 82, widowed 6 years]

> My brother and I are at odds now over the division of our father's Will and I find this very sad. I don't think this division is his fault. It's more a problem for his second wife but he can't go against her. [Woman aged 71, widowed 31 years]

Canadian research has rather consistently found evidence for the emotional bonds between the widowed and members of their "family of origin." These findings are quite in contrast with Lopata's findings in Chicago, where, she notes, children are by far the most viable members of the widow's support system (1978; 1979). Siblings, in-laws, and other relatives were not actively involved in any of the support systems that Lopata studied. Where widows were involved at all in support systems, they were dependent on their children for all types of support except economic.

In the Guelph pilot study, which used the instrument developed by Lopata, over half of the respondents with living siblings saw at least one as frequently as several times a month. More significantly, siblings and other extended kin also emerged as important figures in the social and emotional support systems. In all, 54 percent of the widows listed at least one sibling (typically a sister) as being involved in at least one exchange in the social support system. Sixty-five percent listed an extended-kin member (sibling, sibling-in-law, cousin, aunt, or niece) as involved in their emotional support system. Half the respondents specifically referred to a sister as one of the three people to whom they felt closest, either currently or in the year before their husband's death (Martin Matthews 1982).

There are several possible explanations for the disparate findings in the Guelph pilot study and the Chicago survey. It may be that because a higher proportion of the Canadian widows grew up in their local area than did the Chicago widows, they were able to retain more contacts with siblings and other extended kin over the years. It may also be that because almost half the Chicago widows had at least one child still living at home (in contrast with 15 percent of the widows in the Guelph pilot study), the presence of children made them more salient resources than extended kin at this stage in the life course. It is interesting to note that in another Canadian study focused on the supports of both widowed and non-widowed elderly men and women, siblings were again identified as close family members (Martin Matthews 1987b). There was also evidence of high levels of contact between the widowed and their siblings. Over 82 percent of the widowed and 88 percent of the non-widowed reported regular contact with siblings.

In a study of 50 urban Acadian widows in Moncton, New Brunswick, with a median age of 77 and an average six years of widowhood, Arsenault (1986) found fully 22 percent who identified a sister or other extended kin member (niece, granddaughter, cousin, or in-law) as *the* person most helpful to the widow. Ten percent specifically mentioned a sister in this role. Australian research on the widowed similarly noted that patterns of helping by kin other than children is "dominated by sisters" (McCallum 1986, 144).

Studies of younger widows similarly corroborate the importance of siblings in the lives of the bereaved. Vachon et al. (1980) found evidence of the important supportive role of members of the family of origin, although they do not specify whether or not they were siblings. Similarly, a study of widowed women in Winnipeg, Manitoba, found that median contact with siblings was two or three times per month (Harris and Harvey 1987). Fully 44 percent of a sample of 141 women widowed an average of two years had weekly contact with siblings. The residential stability of these women (a median 35 years residence in Winnipeg) may account in part for the extent of sibling involvement in their supports in widowhood.

Being part of a previously married dyad, as are the widowed or the separated/divorced, is associated with high levels of contact between siblings. In a London, Ontario, study of 400 persons aged 65 or over, 36 percent of whom were widowed, Connidis (1989c, 440) found that the widowed had more active ties with siblings than they had had when married, thus suggesting a pattern of reliance on siblings to compensate for the loss of a spouse.

These findings raise the issue of how potentially supportive sibling ties become when both members of a sibling pair have experienced the loss of the spouse. Connidis (1989c, 440) found high levels of contact between previously married siblings, reflecting "the reservoir of support that is available when the experience of widowhood or divorce is shared with a sibling." Similarly, O'Bryant (1987) found that siblings who served as emotional supports were often widowed and that widowed siblings appeared to serve as "advance role models" who provided a sense of consciousness-of-kind in widowhood (McGloshen and O'Bryant 1988). United States research (Anderson 1984, 1987; O'Bryant 1988) similarly found evidence of strong emotional support between the widowed and their siblings. But there may be limits to the benefits of this level of shared experience. Both O'Bryant (1988) and Connidis (1989c) found that widows may more actively seek the company of married or single sisters than that of widowed sisters, possibly because, as O'Bryant notes, contact between widows is not necessarily morale enhancing.

In order to explore more fully the relationship between sibling ties and widowhood in later life, the Ontario widowhood study explored the issue of sibling relations in some depth. Over two-thirds of the widowed indicated that they were in regular contact with at least one brother or sister; fully 42 percent named siblings, among other relatives, when they defined who meant "family" to them. Indeed, two-thirds considered at least one sibling (usually a sister) a close friend, indicating that the ties are strong between the widowed and at least some of their siblings.

However, on measures of tangible support, a rather different profile emerged. Siblings were rarely involved in the support systems of the widowed in the exchange of assistance. Tables 4.2 and 4.4 in Chapter 4 illustrate 12 types of helping situations about which the widowed were asked. They show that siblings are rarely first choices in terms of many types of support, typically coming well after children and friends. Even in terms of such types of support as having someone with whom to discuss family problems, only 11 percent of the widowed would go first to a sibling. And yet they described their siblings as "very close." These findings are supported by other research. O'Bryant (1987) similarly found that only 22 percent of siblings provided some form of support to the widowed. It may indeed be that the mere presence of siblings as *potential* sources of support is their greatest contribution to the support networks of the widowed, even if their tangible help is rarely sought or received (Cicirelli 1980).

Overall, these research findings indicate that the relative importance of extended family members like siblings varies in relation to the measure of family integration employed. The widowed elderly and their siblings generally express high levels of emotional support, lower levels of frequency of contact, and as might be expected between age peers who are not necessarily geographically proximate, comparatively low levels of tangible support.

THE ROLE OF EXTENDED KIN

While less research attention has been given to ties between the widowed and their extended kin than has been given to ties with other family members, it is clear that such kin play an important role in the lives of some widowed people. Anderson's (1984) research in Nebraska noted the particular reliance placed by the widowed on extended kin in times of personal crisis. Fully 20 percent of the widowed confided in extended kin when they were worried, and 15 percent turned to extended kin when they were depressed. Indeed, the widowed were significantly more likely than the married to report feelings of emotional closeness to their extended kin.

Other research has found that while there are no significant marital status differences in naming peer family (siblings, cousins, aunts, and uncles) as confidants, the widowed are the most likely to name other relatives (grandchildren, nieces/nephews, and second cousins) as confidants, compared with other marital status groups (Strain and Chappell 1982, 493).

This supports other research by Martin Matthews, which has found that the widowed are more likely than the non-widowed elderly (20 percent vs. 14 percent) to identify nieces and nephews in discussions of family relationships. In the Ontario widowhood study, 70 percent of the widowed reported feeling close to extended kin, especially grandchildren, nieces, and nephews. And, as the data to be discussed further in Chapters 4 and 5 show, these "other relatives" were certainly viable members of the support networks of the widowed. In terms of patterns of contact and in terms of the frequency with which they would be called upon as sources of support, particularly on ceremonial occasions and to help resolve family problems, the role of "other relatives" is frequently acknowledged in the support networks of the widowed. As will be examined further in Chapter 4, extended family relations with nieces and nephews in particular may assume special significance in the lives of the childless widowed.

THE ROLE OF FRIENDS AND NEIGHBOURS

The role of friend and neighbour ties in the lives of the widowed elderly may be examined in terms of the continuity of ties throughout the transition to widowhood and the acquisition of new social ties following widowhood. In the latter analysis, friendships among a reference group of other widowed individuals, as well as friendships with members of the opposite sex, are of particular interest.

As suggested in the research by Bankoff reported earlier in this chapter, friendship ties — especially those with married friends — may become quite tenuous in the early period of widowhood when the need is particularly acute for nurturance by someone who can be genuinely empathetic. Particularly because friendship ties are typically based on common interests and lifestyles rather than on feelings of mutual obligation and responsibility, "when a wife becomes a widow, the underlying basis of relationships with married friends is sabotaged, leaving at best an ambiguous basis for continued friendships" (Bankoff 1983b, 836). One strategy for responding to this change in status is to modify one's relationships with married friends into sex-segregated ones (Lopata 1979).

Other studies as well have found friendships to be the crucial relationships most likely to change during bereavement, and this is not merely true of friendships with married people. A primary reason for this is the fact that "friendship is contingent: it depends on the other person's ability to respond to the widow's needs" (Morgan 1989, 105). While families have certain role responsibilities that they are *expected* to fulfil in interaction with a recently widowed person, any friendship, based as it is on reciprocity and mutual need fulfilment, may be strained or terminated if these criteria are not met. In research at the Clark Institute of Psychiatry in Toronto, it was found that many widows had not even seen in several months individuals whom they had previously considered to be close friends. From six months after bereavement, half of the widowed women noted a decrease in social relationships. Indeed, 73 percent of the widows experienced at least one change in their social relationships over the first two years of adaptation to bereavement (Vachon 1981). There was a significant association between the number of relationship changes a woman experienced and her score on a measure of distress. The widows typically responded to changes in social relationships in two ways: the high distress group tended to withdraw in anger and resentment, and became increasingly isolated; the low distress group took these changes as the opportunity to initiate new relationships.

Findings from the Guelph pilot study similarly indicated some attrition in friendships. For 15 percent of the widows, the person who was their closest friend in the year prior to widowhood was no longer a friend at time of interview. The Ontario widowhood study as well found evidence of this phenomenon. A 71-year-old woman widowed eight years reported that she currently had no close friends, noting that "I had friends that I thought were close but when you are widowed and they aren't, they drift away." However, Lopata (1979) did not find this pattern to be particularly pervasive: only 4 percent of friends from prior to widowhood were no longer considered to be friends. Close to 12 percent of old friends had died. Overall, it appears that friendship ties are particularly vulnerable when widowhood occurs as an off-time life event, as when the person is widowed at a young age (see Caine 1974 for an account of such an event) and therefore lacks an appropriate reference group of others who have shared the experience and can express a "consciousness of kind." Particularly in these circumstances, widowed persons lose not only a spouse but also their entrée into a couple-companionate society (Lopata 1979) to which virtually all their friends belong.

In spite of and perhaps even because of the daunting changes that accompany widowhood, new friendships are nevertheless typically acquired. Lopata (1979) reported the acquisition of new friends by 43 percent of her respondents, and they were seen more often on average than any other contact. The change in life circumstance associated with widowhood in later life may even be the impetus for the conscious seeking out of others in similar circumstances (Matthews 1986). In an analysis of the effect of new relationships and activities on the level of distress in widowhood, a significant relationship was found between the development of new friendship relations and bereavement outcome (Vachon 1981). Seventy-six percent of the low distress women had developed new relationships two years after bereavement, compared with 57 percent of the high distress women.

Peer relationships with other widows are also important in the social support networks of the bereaved. In a study of widows living in age-segregated housing in Hamilton, Ontario, the vast majority (92 percent) reported associations limited to other older widows; and 92 percent indicated that their closest friend was also a widow. Typically (in 62 percent of cases) the friendship originated after bereavement. The importance of the friendship role is also confirmed in the finding that "close friendship was the second best significant predictor of the criterion variable, social adjustment" (Elias 1977, 77).

Yet another indicator of the importance of friendship roles in the social support networks of the widowed elderly is the finding that 8 percent of a sample of widowed elderly included at least one friend in descriptions of their "family." Only 4 percent of the non-widowed similarly described a friend as a family member. Fully 76 percent of respondents in a United States study of widows reported close long-lasting friendships, and 40 percent of the widows maintained primary ties exclusively with those whom they had known long before becoming widowed (Babchuk and Anderson 1989). Despite patterns of attrition in friendships upon widowhood, as noted previously, the loyalty factor appears to be important in some friend relationships. Among younger women widowed for five years, a majority expressed the view that old friends cannot be replaced no matter how one tries to make new friends (Harvey and Bahr 1980). In Lopata's (1979) Chicago study, over one-third of the widows kept their old friends but did not develop new ones.

Also germane to discussions of friendship supports is the role of the confidant in the emotional support system of the widowed. In research on emotional supports, Strain and Chappell found no statistically significant differences between the single/separated/divorced, the married, and the widowed in terms of the number of confidants in the emotional support system. Significant differences were apparent, however, in the number of confidants reported by the widowed males and females. The females were more likely than the males to report at least one confidant: 18 percent of the widowed men reported no confidant, but over one-half (54 percent) of the widowed females reported having two or more confidants. This finding that "widowed women...are more likely to have established intimate relationships outside their marriages" (Strain and Chappell 1982, 489) corroborates other Canadian research, such as that of Haas-Hawkings (1978) and others. By contrast, Lopata (1979, 102) found that "a friend was not the main confidante for most widows."

There is some evidence that, compared with married persons, widowed women are more likely to depend on non-kin when worried or depressed. "Being widowed...is related to friends entering older women's emotional support systems" (Anderson 1987, 133). Data from the Ontario widowhood study further indicate that friends are active in the support networks of the widowed (more so than extended kin, for example), and provide support across a range of activities and circumstances (see Tables 4.2, 4.3, 4.4, and 5.1). Overall research findings on the role of friendships in the lives of the widowed are somewhat contradictory. While Lopata (1979) found that the widowed manifest towards friendships cautious attitudes that inhibit the formation of close ties, Lubben (1988) noted the apparent superiority of friends over family as sources of psychological well-being.

The issue of friendships with members of the opposite sex (referred to in the literature as "cross-sex" or "cross-gender" friendships) was of course implicit in the discussions in Chapter 2 of patterns of remarriage following widowhood, but it is also relevant in this context. While over a third of the respondents in the Ontario widowhood study reported a close friend of the opposite sex, most typically this was the spouse of a person with whom the widowed felt especially close. Nevertheless, there were individuals who spoke of a "special" cross-gender friend who provided companionship or served as an escort. Despite the prevalence of cross-gender friendships among the elderly (Knudsen 1988), these were comparatively unusual cases among the widowed. Cross-sex friendships are the exception rather than the norm for both married women and widows (Babchuk and Anderson 1989). And, as noted by Matthews (1986, 91), these friendships "were considered in most cases to be potentially sexual or courtship relationships and therefore essentially different from same-gender relationships in important ways."

Although most studies of the widowed make little distinction between the roles of friends and neighbours, McCallum (1986, 144) observed that while friends engage in supportive relationships "facilitated by commonality of status," neighbours provide "limited practical help which requires proximity but low commitment." But the distinction frequently blurs. In the Guelph pilot study, nearly three-quarters of the respondents identified neighbours as helpful resources to them in bereavement, and over 80 percent identified friends as being similarly helpful (Martin Matthews 1982).

Research on elderly widows living in age-segregated apartment complexes has also emphasized the importance of neighbours as friends and as social supports to the widowed (Elias 1977). Most women in Elias's study had a neighbour who had become a close friend, and about 90 percent of respondents felt that neighbours in the current age-segregated environment were friendlier than those in their previous housing. The majority had made casual friendships with neighbours who lived on the same floor of the building (1977, 62).

THE ROLE OF THE LATE SPOUSE

The issue of the role of the late spouse in the social and emotional supports of the widowed has received some research attention. Lopata (1973b; 1979; 1981) has provided a thorough analysis of the process of "sanctification" of the spouse's memory in widowhood, and has noted that the persistence of memories of the former spouse may have two functions: they may, by comparison, emphasize the negative aspects of the current situation, or they may assist in working through the current situation. Her research has noted the significance of the "memory constructed husband" in the lives of the widowed, "sometimes...providing supports even after death" (Lopata 1979, 75). A Canadian study contrasting the patterns of social involvement of widows and never-married women (see Chapter 5) also found that the widows' higher average score on global measures of involvement was influenced not only by their engagement in activities deriving from their *former* status as spouse (for example, in parenting and grandparenting), but also by their perceived *current* involvement in the role of spouse (Norris 1980). Responses to questions about marriage were frequently phrased as if the husband were still alive. For example, rather than view statements about married life as personally no longer relevant, widowed women frequently expressed strong agreement with the statement "Being married makes my daily activities more satisfying and easy to deal with." "Through an inability or a desire not to relinquish the role, they remained emotionally committed to being wives....Widows....had apparently maintained the central role of their lives, spouse...into old age" (Norris 1980, 142).

These findings suggest that feelings of closeness and the continuance of ties to the deceased play a potentially important role in the lives of the widowed. Thoughts about what a spouse may have said or done in a particular situation may contribute to a sense of continuity between the past and the present. "The tie to the spouse represents a tie to the widow(er)'s own past that cannot or should not be cut" (Ingebretsen 1986). These ties to the past may well extend beyond the former spouse and are by no means exclusive to the widowed. As Unruh (1983, 72) notes,

> Social worlds in aging lives may be rooted in the past, as well as the present...Involvement in activities in which the aged were no longer actively engaged have continued to be sources of integration through memories that provide linkages into social worlds.

The literature contains clinical accounts (cf. Robson 1974) of, for example, a widow writing to her dead husband, "telling him of both the anguish of her loss and of her struggle with her new status, widowhood." While references to the deceased may occupy the conversations of the bereaved (Lehman et al. 1987), and obsessive thoughts of the deceased spouse are common, some authors even suggest that "hallucinations concerning the dead spouse are common..., a normal event in widowhood... [and] may occur for up to ten years after bereavement" (Sawa 1986, 2659-60). Without the benefit of rigorous longitudinal research, it is not possible to determine whether this behaviour is transitory in the experience of widowhood or whether, for some widowed persons, an ongoing relationship with the deceased spouse and continuing identification with the role of spouse serve as meaningful resources throughout widowhood.

THE ROLE OF SELF-HELP AND MUTUAL SUPPORT GROUPS

The term *self-help*, or mutual aid, has a variety of meanings, ranging from individual care to large-scale mutual aid networks. Mutual aid and self-help may take the form of formal or informal support, and in fact self-help groups run the full spectrum, including "social networks emerging from indigenous community groups; advocacy organizations promoting a cause; and groups formed to address common individual problems such as persons with arthritis or families with victims of Alzheimer's disease" (Moody 1985, 32). The character of these groups is, however, frequently informal, often including "a strong share of distrust for experts, scepticism about professional wisdom, and rejection of control by distant corporations or government bureaucracies" (ibid.).

The literature suggests numerous potential benefits derived from self-help groups by those who participate in them. "Participants can gain hope, receive new ideas for solutions, receive information on locating additional sources of help, improve skills in developing social relationships, become less lonely, learn new role definitions, have an audience of listeners, discover that others share similar difficulties and receive added social support" (Lund et al. 1989, 204). Despite the broad support for self-help groups, their effectiveness has not been overwhelmingly established. Nevertheless, research on mutual aid among those experiencing bereavement has noted improvements in terms of nervousness, tiredness, depression, and sleeplessness (Raphael, as reported in Lund et al. 1985). Groups must have well-defined objectives, however. Those which focus exclusively on the "mutual comparison of miseries are less likely to be productive" (Lund et al. 1989, 205).

Perhaps the best known studies of self-help groups among the widowed reflect the work in the United States of Phyllis Silverman, who has focused on linking relationships, the widowed developing interdependent relationships born of shared experiences (Silverman 1986), and on the widowed finding "others like themselves with whom they can identify..., role models that facilitate their learning" (Silverman 1987, 190). National self-help networks such as THEOS in the U.S. and Cruise in the U.K. (DiGiulio, 1989) are based on similar premises.

In Canada, some of the substantial work by Vachon and associates at the Clarke Institute of Psychiatry on the first two years of bereavement has focused on the role of support groups for the widowed. In a two-year study of 162 widows, 68 were paired with a widow contact who provided emotional support and practical assistance. The difference between the widows receiving intervention and the controls at 6, 12, and 24 months after bereavement suggested that those receiving intervention followed the same general course of adaptation as control subjects but that the rate of achieving landmark stages was accelerated for the intervention group (Vachon et al. 1980). However, another self-help group intervention was judged to be only a "qualified success in that women of lower socio-economic status, immigrants and women whose spouse suffered a lengthy final illness were reluctant to participate" (Rogers et al. 1980).

Another current initiative in Canada focuses on the potential of self-help groups for one particular population among the widowed: widowers. Widowers Surviving, sponsored jointly by a Toronto-based medical centre and a funeral home, includes widowers of any age whose spouses have died within the past nine months (Permaul 1990). Small groups meet weekly over a two-month period and discuss such issues as cooking, household management, social life, changes, and new relationships. To date, 10 nine-week support groups have been run with an average of 9 widowers per group. While the evaluation of this programme is still under way, generally it is known that widowers are hesitant to seek emotional and psychological help from any but their closest intimates (Clark et al. 1986). Another Canadian undertaking is Calgary Widowed Services, serving 300 clients per year, approximately 15 of them widowers. Widowed volunteers work either on a one-to-one basis or in weekly support groups, although widowers are more likely to prefer the individual counselling (McLaren 1990). Support groups for widows have existed in British Columbia since 1972 (Cusack 1988).

Such factors as the role of competent and constructive group leaders and the requirements of organization and planning have been identified as important to the success of self-help groups. In addition, potential limitations of self-help groups are that "participants might become too reliant on the group for support and that the groups cannot fully replace other professional and bureaucratic services" (Lund et al. 1989, 205).

Rates of non-participation in self-help groups for the bereaved elderly are a concern for organizers of such programs. Studies by Vachon et al.

(1980) and Rogers et al. (1980) of a Toronto-based widow-to-widow out-reach program reported that 90 percent of those invited to participate agreed to do so, but this figure is unusually high. Some studies report participation rates in therapeutic intervention of only about 4 percent of those who have lost spouses (Lieberman and Videka-Sherman 1986). In a retrospective study of the widowed who wanted an intervention and those who did not, Lund et al. reported that the 44 percent of the sample who wanted an intervention were slightly more likely to be female, younger, more educated, employed, to have been married for fewer years, and to be living in higher income areas, although none of these differences were statistically significant (1989). Nevertheless, there does indeed appear to be some selectivity in terms of the profiles of participants in intervention programs for the widowed. Participants in a national United States support network whose local chapters aid widowed people in their communities were "younger, better educated, more likely to be Protestant, more recently widowed, more likely to be female, and less likely to be remarried than the normative widowed sample" (Lieberman and Videka-Sherman 1986, 439). Recruiting and retaining widowers is a particular challenge for self-help groups, especially in circumstances where there is not a widower counsellor and where widowers may "become overwhelmed by the prospect of being so grossly outnumbered by women" (McCourt, et al. 1976, 100). Even among well-established groups, practical problems in the selection, training, and supervision of leaders (Lund et al. 1989) and the selection of meeting sites (Cusack 1988) must continually be overcome.

EXCHANGES OF AID: SERVICE SUPPORTS

A strong ethic of independence characterizes the widowed in Canada, reflected in a pattern of seeking help only in extraordinary circumstances (Martin Matthews 1987b). Lopata observed a similiar pattern in her research on Chicago-area widows. There is evidence that Canadian widows do not rely extensively on a service support system, reciprocal or otherwise. Only one Canadian study has specifically addressed this aspect of the support networks of widowed women, however, and conclusions must necessarily remain tentative. The Guelph pilot study examined patterns of the receipt and giving of various kinds of service support: transportation, household repairs, help with housekeeping, help with shopping, yard work, child care, sick care, help in decision making, and provision of legal aid (Martin Matthews 1982). While overall there was relatively little involvement in most of these supports, some types of service usage were engaged in by many of the widows. For example, assistance with minor repairs was received by 65 percent of the widowed, yard work by 46 percent, transportation by 43 percent, and legal aid by 42 percent. The areas where assistance was most frequently given to others were transportation (54 percent), help to others in times of illness (46 percent) and child care (35 percent). While these figures indicate the service supports most frequently given to and received by widows, they hardly represent extensive service involvement in the lives of others, for only in one case (assistance received for minor repairs) did a majority of the widows avail themselves of the service.

These figures reflect a somewhat more pervasive pattern of service support than that found by Lopata. Until a more comprehensive examination of the service support systems of Canadian widows is available, however, there is no ready explanation for these differences, particularly in the *giving* of such service supports as the provision of child care (in which 35 percent of the widows in the Guelph pilot study but only 20 percent of the Chicago widows were engaged). Less than 4 percent of the widows in the Guelph pilot study wished for some type of service support that had not materialized (Martin Matthews 1982).

THE ROLE OF FORMAL SUPPORTS

The utilization of services involves not merely the exchange of aid but also the utilization of formal services offered by government or purchased services. A general pattern of underutilization of formal services by the widowed has been well documented in the literature (Lopata 1979; Martin Matthews 1982). A Winnipeg study of the decision-making patterns of middle-aged widows provides some further insight into patterns of usage of formal services. In examining patterns of decision making along a range of issues (car sale/purchase; medical visit; house sale/purchase; job acquisition; car and house repair; husband's estate; relocation; and remarriage), Harris and Harvey found that the widows who had made decisions had only infrequently sought help in arriving at a course of action. The cases where support in decision making was sought most typically involved car sale or purchase (52 percent) and the spouse's estate (55 percent). Decisions about medical visits and remarriage rarely involved consultation with others (11 percent and 8 percent respectively) (Harris and Harvey 1987).

A study of 298 widowed women in Melbourne, Australia, by Roseman et al. (1981) also found relatively little use of organized social services for personal problems. Where the professional support network was utilized at all, it most typically involved persons with whom the widowed would have had contact in other circumstances, such as bank managers and teachers. There was no evidence of seeking specifically trained professionals such as social workers to deal with issues of widowhood.

The reasons for underutilization of services are not entirely clear. In documenting low use of formal services among the rural elderly, Scott and Roberto (1985) noted a lack of perceived need, negative attitudes towards receipt of assistance, fear of loss of independence, and little understanding of bureaucratic procedures. O'Bryant and Morgan (1990) reported moderate to high self-sufficiency among the widowed and supported the notion of an ethic of independence among a sample of recently widowed women.

One potentially important member of the formal support system of the widowed is the physician. However, the actual role of physicians in the support systems of the widowed has not been well investigated, and research findings are rather contradictory. The physician frequently bears the responsibility for informing family members of a death, and can provide "anticipatory guidance" (Sawa 1986, 2661) to reduce the trauma of bereavement. This may involve providing accurate information, facilitating opportunities for interaction with the dying person, permitting contributions to the care of the patient, and being sensitive to the need to express emotions (Sawa 1986). The role of the physician after the actual widowhood is less clear. While there is a belief that "the physician is a potential source of valuable support, one who can help the widow understand which physical symptoms are normal and which are not" (DiGiulio 1989, 63), there is limited empirical evidence of this. In the pioneering study of widows in London, Marris (1958) referred to physicians as being frequent targets of anger among recently bereaved widows. In Lopata's study of 1,169 Chicago-area widows, no mention was made whatever of the role of physicians in the support system, even though the widows had no fewer than 195 opportunities to list any given individual as a potential supporter.

The role of the physician in the supports of the widowed elderly was specifically examined in a British study by Bowling and Cartwright (1982). Data were collected not only from individuals widowed less than six months but also, in 39 percent of cases, from their physicians (specifically, general practitioners). Such characteristics of the general practitioners as the nature of their medical training, attitudes towards the aged, and knowledge of the widowed's household and family circumstances were examined in relation to the type of care given to the widowed. Through the examination of the different perspectives that different players (the widowed, their family members, and their physicians) have of the same events, the data indicated that in general the widowed themselves are less critical of their physicians than are their family members. While two-fifths of the physicians thought that elderly people should be visited at home when they were widowed and most thought this should be done as soon as possible, less than a quarter of the elderly widowed had in fact been visited by a general practitioner after their spouse died but before the funeral.

Perhaps the most disturbing finding relates to the physicians' lack of knowledge of drug use by their widowed patients. If the information from the widowed individuals themselves was accurate, then doctors were aware that only about half as many of their patients were taking minor tranquillizers as were actually doing so. The physicians defined by the widowed as "unsympathetic" were most likely to prescribe psychotropic drugs to the recently widowed. Despite findings of "a tendency to prescribe pills rather than give supportive care to the bereaved" (Bowling and Cartwright 1982, 223), these authors argue that general practitioners, even more than clergy, social workers, or other community support workers, have a particular responsibiiity to help depressed, apathetic, and isolated widows and widowers, and "should be encouraged and stimulated to perform this role more adequately than they do at present" (Bowling and Cartwright 1982, 228–29).

A Canadian study of 21 men widowed an average of 11 months found increased use of family physician services and concluded that such visits could be used more effectively among the widowed if physicians provided more counselling services and were better able to make full use of community organizations to minimize the isolation of elderly widowers (Tudiver 1988, 299). Research suggests overall that "family physicians are usually poorly equipped to deal with conjugal bereavement in the elderly" (Tudiver 1986, 2700).

There is little empirical evidence of a strong supportive role played by other members of the "helping professions." Indeed, the "surprising, dramatic failure" of clergy in the support systems of widows was noted by Lopata (1979, 251), who observed that priests, ministers, or rabbis were not deemed to be supportive to the widowed either during the husband's illness, immediately after his death, in the "life-rebuilding stage or at the present time....The absence of religious advisors from these supports is startling considering the supportive nature of religious promises." In contrast, British research found that, among the recently widowed, nearly half had been visited by a member of the clergy. Most of those visited found the visit helpful, and those visited scored somewhat higher on a measure of adjustment than did those who were not visited by clergy (Bowling and Cartwright 1982). Harris and Harvey (1987) similarly found that while seeking help from "professional listeners" was rare among widows, those who were sought out by the widows tended to be ministers.

While clergy themselves may not necessarily play a particularly supportive role in the lives of the widowed, the importance of religious involvement or religious belief has been noted by several researchers. McGloshen and O'Bryant (1988) found that frequency of attendance at worship services was significantly related to positive affect among the widowed, while Wortman and Silver (1990, 256) suggested that "an individual's religious orientation, or view of the world, may be particularly likely to serve as a protective function against the initial, potentially devastating effects of conjugal bereavement."

Although not systematically investigated in studies of the widowed, funeral directors were identified as "a great help" by fully 76 percent of a sample of bereaved men and women in a U.S. study (Carey 1979–1980).

Beyond specific services directed to the widowed, however, there are more generic formal supports that the widowed may access. In recent years many services have been developed to promote independence among the community-dwelling elderly, including the widowed, by providing assistance with their daily personal and domestic activities. Forbes et al. noted that "up to 12 percent of elderly living in the community need assistance with activities such as dressing, washing and preparing a meal, and as many as 25 percent need help with housework and shopping" (1987, 48). Home care and homemaker services are the primary vehicles throughout Canada by which these services are provided to the elderly by someone other than a relative or friend.

The proliferation of in-home community-based services does appear to be benefiting the widowed. As one example, the elderly living alone (most of them widowed) constitute 48 percent of all clients of visiting homemaker programmes in Ontario (Canadian Council on Homemaker Services 1982). For many such individuals, a home care programme such as homemaker services serves "primarily as a nursing home bed replacement or postponement program helping the elderly remain at home as long as possible" (Shapiro 1986, 40). These services continue, however, to be utilized by only a minority of the elderly widowed. Lopata's (1979, 355) observation of "the failure of widows to use many of the supports deemed beneficial in the modern urban environment" is largely corroborated by research findings.

THE SELF AS RESOURCE

Before leaving the issue of social supports in widowhood, it is important to acknowledge how the personal resources of the widowed person influence both the extent of the social supports utilized and also the response to and attitude towards available social supports. Lopata has recognized that the widow "needs to make herself over, from a dependent person, living vicariously through the husband and children, into an independent person" (1979, 32) and that "many of the women are aware of themselves as a resource to supply supports" (1979, 75). Similarly, for elderly widowers, the loss of the spouse frequently necessitates the learning of domestic skills (Wister and Strain 1986) and the negotiation of family and friend linkages formerly maintained by their wife (Kohn and Kohn 1978; Rosenthal 1987).

As previously discussed, widowhood is associated with many changes in the attitudes and behaviours of others in relation to the bereaved person. Adult children, especially daughters, may assume more nurturing and supportive roles; siblings may become emotionally closer; friendships with members of married couples may become attenuated and gradually replaced by new friends who share a sense of consciousness of kind with the widowed; a primary significant other, the spouse, is lost in fact but retained — albeit selectively — in memory. This redefinition in the attitudes and behaviours of others will, as discussed in Chapter 1, contribute to the redefinition of the me, of the widowed person's sense of herself or himself.

Recalling the conceptualization of widowhood in Chapter 1 as involving the "stepping into a new world," we recognize it also to be true that the widowed person stepping into that unfamiliar world is essentially a "new person." In this section, we will consider how the widowed construct their own action in relation to their support networks, and not merely how they respond to them.

Much research examines social supports without any consideration of the personal resources that the widowed bring to the support relationship, resources that provide a context for interpreting the meaning of that support. However, awareness of changes in personal resources (feelings of independence, confidence, and freedom; employment; and the ability to drive) has significant implications for how the widowed view their social supports (Martin Matthews 1982, 229), and for how they utilize societal and community resources (Lopata 1979).

Lopata's studies are among the few that address this issue. In her early research, Lopata found that over half the widowed women felt that they had personally been changed by the experience of widowhood (Lopata 1973a; 1973b). In subsequent research she found that many widows were aware of themselves as a resource supplying supports. Typical was the widow who "sees herself as the major provider of a self-feeling such as independence or self-sufficiency, being obviously pleased that she is able to obtain this support from herself" (Lopata 1979, 75). In comparing sources of social, financial, service, and emotional support before and after widowhood, Lopata found that after bereavement there were more contributions to the support network by "self" or "no one." She concluded that this indicates two different kinds of widows, one type who gains self-confidence and positive feelings about the self after having survived widowhood, while the other "becomes desolated by these events" (Lopata 1979, 259). Other research on participants of widow(er) support groups has similarly found that many widowed persons seem "to develop another side of themselves" and are transformed by the process of adaptation to widowhood (Silverman 1987, 189).

In order to explore further this issue of the reconstruction of self in widowhood, the Ontario widowhood study incorporated several questions that allowed for an extensive discussion of the widowed individual's personal supports. Previous experience in the Guelph pilot project (Martin Matthews 1982) had indicated that such discussions provide valuable insight into self-perception among the widowed. There are distinctly different contexts in which the change in social support in widowhood takes place, is interpreted, and has meaning for these widows. Some widows felt bitter, others resigned, others quite invigorated by their own adaptability and resilience—all quite different *interpretations* of changes in their support systems following widowhood (Martin Matthews 1982; 1987a).

Data from the Ontario widowhood study further illustrate this point.

The extent of changes in self accompanying widowhood have been discussed in Chapter 2. Some individuals spoke poignantly of their loss as "the worst thing that ever happened to me," and described their new life in terms such as "much quieter now"; "I don't have the same interest." Others, while experiencing a genuine sense of loss, observed; "However, you have to make the best of it. You can't give up. The more you help others, the more you forget about your own problems" (Woman aged 63, widowed 5 years). "You have to accept that the person is gone, not coming back. I don't spend my time wishing him back. You have to learn to tie your own shoelace and get going. Don't feel 'poor me'" (Woman aged 62, widowed 3 years). Such responses indicate a determination on the part of widows to overcome their bereavement, to make the best of bereavement as an opportunity for growth and development.

These findings suggest the need for research on widowhood to examine more fully the social *meaning* of widowhood for women and men. The social reconstruction of self in widowhood is central to this meaning. For some, widowhood may indeed be "a role fully defined by the absence of something — by 'nothingness'" (DiGiulio 1989, 57). The widowed remain "'the widow of' or substitute other people for the late husband as sources of identity and other emotional supports" (Lopata 1979, 294). But for others, the role changes associated with widowhood are accompanied by a more positive reconstruction, a new defining of oneself as a "partnerless person" (Lopata 1979), seeing oneself as a contributor to the support network. In any study of changes in patterns of social support in widowhood, the possibility of change in the widowed themselves as an influencing factor must be considered.

CONCLUSION

The role, function, and meaning of social support has been extensively examined in the gerontological literature. There is strong empirical evidence of a positive relationship between social support and health. In studies specifically of widowhood, the primary questions of social support ask who participates in the support systems of the widowed and whether this support makes any difference.

The need for support in widowhood is by no means fixed. Thus the types and sources of support beneficial at one point in widowhood may not necessarily be appropriate at a later point in the transition. Researchers have also questioned the assumption of the inherent value of social support. There is evidence, for example, that low-density networks may be more appropriate in enabling the widowed to develop new social roles consistent with their new status.

The roles of specific members of the support networks of the widowed were a focus of this chapter. Adult children provide most of the care received by older widowed parents. But patterns of contact between the widowed and their adult children are not necessarily uniform, either across children or in terms of the duration of widowhood. Most contact is by daughters, and while the support of adult children is crucial during acute grief, it may become less important over time as friends increase in importance.

Sibling relations hold a unique place in the support network in terms of their longer duration in comparison with other family ties and their essentially egalitarian nature. The research literature shows strong patterns of emotional support between the widowed and their siblings, especially sisters, although frequency of contact and exchange of aid may be comparatively low. Other extended-family members, such as nieces and nephews, also act as viable members of the support networks of the widowed, especially in terms of emotional support. Research has also found that "a husband in memory can also provide a form of support" (Lopata 1979, 352).

Friendship relations evidence substantial change with widowhood. Not distinguished by feelings of obligation that characterize family relations, friendships — especially those with members of a married couple — may not survive widowhood. The ability to make new friendships may indeed be an important indicator of how an individual is coping with the loss of the spouse. Self-help and mutual support groups represent particular kinds of peer relationships. Although typically utilized by only a minority of the widowed, such groups have been demonstrated to effectively reduce the distress of the widowed in intervention groups. Formal organizational supports are consistently underutilized by the widowed.

In relation to all these sources of support, the redefined personal resources of the widowed person will strongly influence the utilization of potential social supports. In any study of changes in patterns of social support in widowhood, the possibility of change in the widowed themselves as an influencing factor must be considered.

Overall, the findings of this chapter corroborate statements of the predominant role of the family as the major force in the informal helping network and as a major player in the overall social support system (Coward 1987). However, it should be noted that research has found fully one in five of the widowed to report not having a single living relative to whom they felt particularly close (Anderson 1987). Clearly, there are many sources of variability in the experience of widowhood, all of which will influence the patterns of access to available social supports and their perceived benefit. Comparisons and contrasts between men and women, and between the rural and the urban widowed, are among the sources of variability discussed in Chapter 4.

CHAPTER 4

VARIABILITY IN THE EXPERIENCE OF WIDOWHOOD

INTRODUCTION

On the societal level, many factors influence the social integration and support systems of widows. Modern societies offer a wide variety of resources for social engagement in the form of personal relations, social groups, and human services agencies (Lopata 1979, 8). The social world within which the relations and roles of a person are located can be concentrated in one institution, as in the family, or it can be multidimensional, as in the case of the widowed mother who is also an involved citizen, neighbour, churchgoer, and so forth. In addition, different socio-economic statuses make available or constrict the social roles available to the widowed. The community within which the widowed are located also plays a role in delineating their status. As Lopata (1979) has noted, not all aspects of the societal and cultural systems are available as resources in every community.

As previous chapters have suggested, the experience of widowhood in later life is associated with a very heterogeneous population whose involvement in social supports is highly variable. This chapter considers several of the sociodemographic factors that contribute both to the diversity of the widowed population and to the social supports available to them and the networks in which they engage. These include issues of gender, residential environment, parental status, ethnicity and culture, and financial resources.

GENDER COMPARISONS

Earlier chapters have noted the dramatic differences in the likelihood of men and women becoming and remaining widowed. These demographic realities imply different circumstances for men and for women in widowhood. Because widows so outnumber widowers and are, as a group, younger on average, they are more likely to have same-sex widowed friends both prior to and during their own widowhood, who may serve as role models and offer social support. On the other hand, the option to remarry is more accessible to widowed men.

63

The greater expectability of widowhood for women than for men frequently becomes translated, at the social-psychological level, into a kind of anticipatory socialization for widowhood that women more readily express throughout their adult lives. For example, a study of women's experiences of residential relocation noted the frequency with which women in middle age would discuss the prospect of being alone in later life. Such comments as the following were typical: "I don't know where I'd go if something happened to my husband"; "If something happened to my husband, I wouldn't stay here" (Martin Matthews 1980a, 272). It is clear from these comments that for many women the prospect of widowhood is a reality they recognize and incorporate as part of their "life plan" (Berger et al. 1973, 73). As a result, their thinking, if not their overt behaviour, frequently involves a mental rehearsal or anticipation of circumstances associated with becoming and being "unattached" later in life. This is a form of anticipatory socialization for widowhood that distinguishes men's and women's images of their own aging. Widowhood is an expectable life event for women, but not for men. This expectability would appear to belie the finding, reported in Chapter 2, of the experience of widowhood as a critical life event. It seems that while women may acknowledge the potentiality of widowhood, this recognition does not lessen the socio-emotional impact of the actual event. As noted in the journal of a widow writing to her late husband in the months following her bereavement: "When you said 'What if I died?' I had no conception of what it meant and no one can, any more than you can imagine a baby if you haven't had one, the mind isn't capable — just as well" (Robson 1974, 222).

The few studies that consider men's experiences of widowhood have typically focused on a debate about whether the transition to widowhood is more difficult for women or for men. Berardo (1970), Barrett (1978), Elwell and Maltbie (1978), and Parkes (1986) are among those who have concluded that widowhood is more stressful for men. Atchley (1975), however, found that widowers were better off than widows on all dimensions, particularly because they have economic supports that for the most part tend to offset the effects of other social and psychological factors. Evidence for the more disadvantaged position of the widower in old age is nevertheless reflected in the findings of higher suicide rates (Bock and Webber 1972) and a greater increase in the rate of mortality following bereavement (Parkes et al. 1969) in comparison with widows.

However, a more fruitful approach to the examination of this issue lies in exploring the ways in which the experience differs for men and women, rather than merely determining for whom the transition is more difficult. Certainly, in terms of access to social support, there is evidence of substantial male-female differences in the transition to widowhood. Widowers are more likely to be isolated and to have fewer emotional ties with their families (Berardo 1970; Pihlblad et al. 1972). Widows, by contrast, apparently become closer to their children, if only for a short time, following bereavement. In addition, while older widows have an available group of other widows to provide emotional and social support, widowers by and large lack such supports. Widowers may be especially disadvantaged because of the tendency for men not to develop confidant relationships with others outside their marital relationships in the way that women frequently do (Lowenthal and Haven 1968). On the other hand, Silverman (1987) has found that, for most men, the sense of who they are is not as intimately tied to their role of husband.

To some extent, the lack of international and Canadian data on widowers is a function of the demography of widowhood. Studies of the widowed often result in samples that are only about 13 percent males, "too few cases to make meaningful comparisons" with widows (Fengler and Danigelis 1982). In the Ontario widowhood study, there were 128 widows but only 24 widowers, again an insufficient sample size for comprehensive analysis.

In spite of these limitations, there are several Canadian studies that compare the experiences of widows and widowers. Stryckman (1981a; 1981b; 1982) has studied 475 widowed men and women, aged 55 and over, living in urban and rural environments in Quebec. Forty-one percent of the sample was male. Stryckman found no difference between men and women in their identification of widowhood as a painful life event (1982, 75), although the sample did not include individuals who had experienced a sudden death of the spouse. The experience of pain did, however, lead to different attitudes towards remarriage, with painfulness linked to the desire to remarry among men and the desire not to remarry among women, as noted in Chapter 2.

The problems of widowhood also differed for men and for women. While loneliness was the major problem for both genders (expressed by 56 percent of the men and 52 percent of the women), financial resources were the second major problem for women but not for men. Widowers found problems with the completion of daily household tasks and with sexuality to be their major areas of concern (Stryckman 1982, 79). An additional difference between the genders was that widows were more likely than widowers to report high frequency of contact with children (1982, 79).

There is also evidence of significant gender differences among the widowed in patterns of confidant relations. As noted in Chapter 3, a Winnipeg study found significant differences in the number of confidants reported by widows and widowers, with the widows reporting many more. Another Winnipeg study examined dimensions of social support among 354 elderly individuals: 42 widowers and 177 widows who used home care services and 24 widowers and 111 widows who did not. Social support was measured by the variables: number of household members; number of relatives outside the home; number of friends outside the home; number of neighbours and number of confidants; frequency of interaction with relatives, friends, and neighbours. Among the non-users of home support services, the widows had more friends and confidants and more interaction with relatives and neighbours than did widowers. Among the users of home support services — an older and more functionally disabled group — the widowers had almost twice as many neighbours on whom they could rely as did the widows. Other statistically significant differences between the genders emerged on the other support measures when controls were introduced: both for those widowed six years or more and those with high functional ability, widows had more frequent interaction than did widowers with relatives and neighbours. In addition, when age was controlled for (comparing those ±80), widows had more interaction with neighbours and more confidants than did widowers. For the users of home support services, however, gender overall made very little difference to the availability and utilization of the specified social supports (Wister and Strain 1986).

These findings suggest a conclusion similar to Scott and Kivett's (1985). In an examination of the effect of sex differences on the morale of older widowed individuals, Scott and Kivett found that economic and physical resources (self-rated health) rather than gender *per se* appeared to be more influential determinants of morale. The findings of Wister and Strain similarly suggest that, with advancing age and increasing functional disability, the similarities between widows and widowers far outweigh the differences.

Gender differences among the widowed emerged in the Ontario widowhood study. For purposes of this analysis, a subsample of 24 of the 128 widows was selected for comparison with the 24 widowers, matched on the basis of length of widowhood (average 7 years), age (average 73 years), and self-reported health status (both groups reporting no health limitations). While the widows and widowers were compared on a range of variables related to perception of social support, social network configuration, health status, and marital history, only statistically significant relationships or relationships where expected differences did not emerge are reported here.

There were no statistically significant differences between the *total* sample of widows and the widowers on various domain-specific measures of life satisfaction, on their perceptions of the relative impact of widowhood on their lives, or on their levels of involvement in social organizations. While widows and widowers expressed similar levels of morale on the overall measure of the Philadelphia Geriatric Center Morale Scale (Lawton 1972), widowers differed from widows in their response to the item that stated: "I sometimes feel that life isn't worth living." Twenty-one percent of the widowers but only 6 percent of the widows agreed with this statement.

The lack of gender differences on many of these social-psychological dimensions was surprising, for other research suggests substantial differences between the genders on these dimensions. While widows have been observed to emerge from the early bereavement period rather worse off than widowers, follow-up studies two to four years later indicated that widows returned to levels of adjustment equivalent to married women of the same age more readily than did widowers to an equivalent control group. "It seems, therefore, that while overt manifestations of grief were more pronounced in women than men during the first year of bereavement, it was the women who were the first to recover from bereavement" (Parkes 1986, 230).

Although some studies find no gender variability in processes of coping with bereavement (Gallagher et al. 1989), Silverman (1987) concluded that there were indeed significant differences between men and women in the way they accommodated to the death of their spouse. In an insightful review of studies of widowhood support groups, she concluded that in the process of adaptation to widowhood, "women seem to become more decisive and self-reliant and the men more caring" (Silverman 1987, 174). While the women seemed to "move to positions of greater autonomy, the men seemed to take more responsibility for their relationships" (ibid, 189). An appreciation of the nature of these changes is important. As Ferraro (1989, 79) has noted, because widowhood is normative for women and not for men, the structure of their networks will necessarily vary, and thus "what appears as a gender difference may, in fact, be a social support difference." Let us now consider these social support differences.

In the Ontario widowhood study, gender comparisons were also made of patterns of social support. As these comparisons were also made for the rural and urban widowed, and as described in Chapter 5, for the different marital status groups, they are described in detail here. Three aspects of social support were measured: patterns of support, sources of support, and perceptions of support.

Patterns of support were measured in terms of the frequency and type of interaction with specific individuals. Although such measures admittedly represent "very crude assessments of the nature of individuals' social worlds, simple measures of the existence and quantity of social relationships are relatively objective, reliable, and not artificially confounded with measures of other relevant variables such as stress and health" (House and Kahn 1985, 90). The frequency of contact with such potential supports as adult children, siblings, and friends was counted, recording patterns of both face-to-face and telephone contacts. In addition, Cantor's (1979) definition of functional support was utilized. As Cantor notes, merely possessing one or more support elements does not necessarily guarantee that older people will receive meaningful support; rather, the issue is whether there are ongoing relationships steady enough to make meaningful support a possibility. Gibbs has similarly found that it is not the number of persons in social support groups but rather "the number of persons available and frequently engaged in social interaction with the widow that is of greater moment in explaining the perceived salience of social relations in widowhood" (1980, 233). In the Ontario widowhood study, functional support was measured on the basis of frequency of contact, varying by type of contact. The criterion was: for child, sibling, other relative, and friend contact, frequency of at least once a month for face-to-face contact *or* frequency of at least once a week for telephone contact.

The sources of social support are conceptualized in terms of the role relationships (kin and non-kin) of those on whom the widowed rely for a variety of supports. Several models exist that attempt to explain the basis on which the elderly select supporters for specific tasks (Peters et al. 1987). A given supporter may perform randomly chosen tasks (an additive model), as when a neighbour occasionally helps purchase groceries, gives legal advice, and so forth. One supporter may dominate all forms of support (asymmetrical model), as when a daughter is the only person a widow will call on for any type of support. Support may vary by the nature of the task (task specific model), as when children always provide emotional support but friends provide tangible support. Conversely, support may vary according to the primacy of the relationship of the support giver to the elderly recipient rather than to the nature of the task (hierarchical-compensatory model) (Cantor 1979, 453). For example, neighbours or acquaintances may be asked for assistance in comparatively "unimportant" situations requiring the changing of a light bulb or the mailing of a letter, while requests of support from children will be saved for more "important" or "personal" matters. However, if children become temporarily or permanently unable to perform these functions, others may be asked to provide supports in their absence.

In order to test these models, the elderly widowed in the Ontario study were asked about whom they preferred as support agents in a series of hypothetical typical life situations. These included situations dealing with such instrumental issues as requiring assistance in getting to the doctor, financial assistance, help in tasks of daily living, and expressive assistance relating to such matters as family problems.

The measure of the perception of support focuses on whether interpersonal relationships serve particular functions (such as providing affection, feelings of belonging, or material aid) and typically ask individuals about their perceptions of the availability or adequacy of resources provided by others (Cohen and Syme 1985). Comparatively few studies have attempted to measure social support in terms of the functional content of social relationships as opposed to their mere existence or structure, and there is little uniformity in the measurement of this concept. In the Ontario widowhood study, the perception of social support was measured by means of the Interpersonal Support Evaluation List (ISEL) (Cohen et al. 1984). This instrument provides an overall measure of perceived support, as well as scores on four subscales that measure self-esteem, appraisal, tangible, and belonging support. The self-esteem subscale measures the availability of someone to promote a sense of self-worth; appraisal assesses the availability of a confidant and advisor; belonging measures the perceived availability of companionship; and the measure of tangible support includes the availability of material aid and service support.

Throughout Chapters 4 and 5, data on these three aspects of support (patterns, sources, and perception of support) as measured in the Ontario widowhood study are used to inform the analysis of gender comparisons, rural-urban variability, and comparisons between the widowed and other marital status groups.

Widows and widowers were compared in terms of the perceived availability of social support. There were *no* differences between widows and widowers in the perception of overall support, or on any of the four subscales measuring self-esteem, appraisal, tangible, and belonging support. Rather surprisingly, given the many indications in the literature of the greater social desolation of widowers than widows, men *and* women in the Ontario study reported relatively high levels of perceived social support.

There were, however, significant differences between the *total* sample of widows and widowers on several individual items on the ISEL, differences that are masked when the responses are summed for the subscales and the overall measure. Widowers were significantly more likely to perceive the availability of someone to offer advice and suggestions about recreational activities, someone with whom to go out for a social evening on short notice, someone who could provide a quick emergency loan of $100 when needed, and someone to provide an early morning ride to the airport. Fully 17 percent of the widowers, but less than 1 percent of the widows, perceived the availability of "someone who takes pride in my accomplishments," a question that a substantial number of widows had difficulty answering.

There were some significant differences between widows and widowers on the patterns of social support, as illustrated in Table 4.1. Comparisons were made incorporating Cantor's (1979) definition of functional supports, as just described. Overall, widows reported significantly more functional extended-family members (such as nieces, nephews, cousins, and grand-children) than did widowers, and more functional people in their networks in total. The numbers of functional siblings, children, and friends did not vary by gender.

The actual patterns (frequency and type) of contact with family and friends also differed for widows and widowers. Males reported significantly more children with whom they had face-to-face contact than did females. This difference between widows and widowers is accounted for by different patterns of contact with the *eldest* child only. Fully 64 percent of widowers but only 32 percent of widows reported that the most typical method of contact with the eldest child was face-to-face. This is largely because widowers were more likely than widows to live with their eldest child (13 percent versus 3 percent). Widows, on the other hand, reported significantly more children and friends with whom they had telephone contact.

TABLE 4.1

PATTERNS OF SOCIAL SUPPORT IN WIDOWHOOD: GENDER COMPARISONS

Measure	Widowers n = 24		Widows n = 24	
	X̄	s.d.	X̄	s.d.
Numbers of Supporters				
Functional Children	1.8	1.1	1.1	1.4
Functional Siblings	0.7	1.0	1.2	1.6
Functional Relatives *	0.5*	1.0	1.3*	1.6
Functional Friends	1.0	1.2	1.4	1.5
Total Functional Contacts *	3.9*	2.6	5.7*	2.5
Face-to-Face Contacts				
Children *	1.3*	1.1	0.6*	0.9
Siblings	1.0	1.5	0.9	1.3
Other Relatives	0.9	1.4	1.2	1.4
Friends	0.9	1.2	0.5	0.7
Total	4.1	3.2	3.2	2.3
Telephone Contacts				
Children *	1.0*	1.3	2.2*	2.3
Siblings	0.8	1.2	1.4	1.6
Other Relatives	0.4	0.8	0.9	1.1
Friends *	0.5*	1.0	1.3*	1.6
Total *	2.6*	2.1	5.7*	3.8

* $p \leq .05$

Overall, widows reported significantly more total telephone contacts with members of their social networks than did males, a pattern that may reflect the transportation difficulties reported by many widows, particularly those living in rural areas and without a driver's licence.

There were two patterns of significant differences between widows and widowers in sources of support, as illustrated in Table 4.2. For tasks that involved discussing family problems, seeking advice, and being made to feel worthwhile (in short, tasks associated with appraisal and self-esteem support), widowers were much more likely to rely primarily on children, and widows on a wider variety of supporters, especially friends/neighbours and other relatives.

For tasks that involved seeking a companion for a walk, for shopping, and for company for the holidays (tasks associated with belonging support), widowers were much more likely to rely on themselves or no one else, and widows on friends and neighbours. Here, it appears, the more extensive networks of the widowed woman provided more alternatives for her. For the one task associated with tangible support for which there was a

TABLE 4.2

PREFERRED SOURCES OF SUPPORT IN WIDOWHOOD: GENDER COMPARISONS[a]

Situation Requiring Support		Self %	Child %	Sibling %	Friend/ Neighbour %	Other Relative %	Informal Org. %	Formal Org. %	Other %	No Answer %
Sick/dizzy at home	Male	4.2	33.3	—	33.3	4.2	8.3	16.7	—	—
	Female	10.9	37.5	6.3	22.7	3.1	3.9	14.8	—	0.8
Ride to doctor	Male	12.5	29.2	—	41.7	4.2	12.5	—	—	—
	Female	7.8	25.0	2.3	28.9	7.0	25.8	2.3	—	0.8
Help after accident	Male	—	16.7	—	—	4.2	4.2	66.7	—	8.3
	Female	—	10.2	3.9	3.1	5.5	—	73.4	—	3.9
Change light bulb	Male	62.5	4.2	—	12.5	8.3	4.2	4.2	—	4.2
	Female	40.6	11.7	—	13.3	14.1	18.0	0.8	—	1.6
Fill out form*	Male	20.8	16.7	—	12.5	4.2	—	41.7	—	4.2
	Female	22.7	35.9	0.8	10.2	10.9	—	19.5	—	—
Look after house	Male	8.3	29.2	—	54.2	—	8.3	—	—	—
	Female	2.3	23.4	2.3	52.3	6.3	5.5	3.1	—	4.7
Discuss family problem*	Male	16.7	54.2	—	8.3	8.3	—	4.2	4.2	4.2
	Female	7.8	22.7	12.5	25.8	16.4	—	11.7	0.8	2.3
Advice/decision*	Male	4.2	70.8	—	4.2	—	—	16.7	4.2	—
	Female	11.7	41.4	1.6	10.9	11.7	—	20.3	—	2.3
Companion for walk*	Male	58.3	4.2	—	20.8	8.3	—	—	8.3	—
	Female	25.8	3.9	2.3	50.8	3.9	0.8	1.6	1.6	9.4
Companion for shopping*	Male	33.3	12.5	8.3	29.2	—	—	—	—	16.7
	Female	7.8	19.5	6.3	48.4	12.5	—	1.6	—	3.9
Company for holidays*	Male	8.3	66.7	—	16.7	4.2	—	—	—	4.2
	Female	1.6	27.3	3.1	25.8	41.4	—	—	—	0.8
Feel worthwhile*	Male	12.5	25.0	—	29.2	12.5	4.2	4.2	—	12.5
	Female	3.9	10.2	2.3	45.3	23.4	2.3	9.4	0.8	2.3

[a] Preferred sources indicated as first choice.
*$p < .05$

significant male/female difference (filling out a form), men were most likely to utilize a formal organization, and women to enlist the help of an adult child.

These data suggest quite different patterns for widows and for widowers of accessing supports. Among the widows, there was evidence of a hierarchical-compensatory model (Cantor 1979) for the utilization of supports, with the women relying primarily on different kinds of supporters (depending on their availability) for different kinds of tasks. Among widowers, however, the model of utilization more closely approximated the asymmetrical model, with the men relying almost exclusively on themselves or their children in most support-seeking situations. Among both widows and widowers, there was evidence of a general reluctance to utilize formal organizations as appropriate avenues for seeking support in relation to personal, financial, or family problems, corroborating similar conclusions drawn by Cantor (1979) and Lopata (1979).

The respondents in this study were also asked whether they *felt* men or women were more disadvantaged by widowhood. There was a significant difference between widows and widowers in their perceptions.

> It's harder for men. A lot of men have never cooked or done housework and their hands are empty. A woman has always had things to do. [Woman aged 77, widowed 5 years]

> It's harder for women. Men can get companionship any time they want. It's harder for a woman to do this without people talking. [Man aged 73, widowed 26 years]

> It all depends on the person. My father could not make himself a cup of tea. I can look after myself. It makes a difference if a woman can't drive. If she never learned to drive she is really handicapped, and a lot of women don't drive. [Man aged 85, widowed 8 years]

Fully 92 percent of the women but only 38 percent of the men thought that widowhood was more difficult for men. The most frequent reason women gave for this perception was male inexperience with household tasks. These respondents, the widows in particular, strongly supported Berardo's (1985, 41) view that the current cohort of elderly men represent "a generation of husbands heavily dependent upon their spouses for physical, emotional, and other kinds of support." Other reasons include: the difficulty men have in socializing, their inexperience with being alone, the lack of male hobbies to occupy time, and the "emotional weakness" of men. The perceived greater disadvantages of widowhood for women included their lower financial resources and inexperience in handling money, the inability of many elderly women to drive, and the social restrictions placed on women.

Overall, these data present a rather bleak portrait of the aged widower in terms of his access to familial and social resources. This conclusion is generally supported in other literature on social supports and adaptation to bereavement as well. In gender comparisons of the married and the widowed elderly, Lubben (1988) found that, although there were no differences between widows and married women in patterns of family contact, widowers were twice as likely as married men to report having neither seen nor heard from a family member in the previous month. McCallum (1986) found that widowers were twice as likely as widows to mention loneliness as a difficulty. Given that widowers have high mortality rates, "the gloomy findings...become even more compelling when one realizes that they are based on the relatively healthy survivors who could be studied in the surveys" (Hyman 1983, 15). Let us now turn to another source of variability in the experience of widowhood, that of residential location.

RURAL-URBAN DIFFERENCES

Several researchers (Fengler and Danigelis 1982; Adams 1975) have noted the particular salience of the environmental context for the aged, and the special vulnerability of the elderly widowed to environmental influence. Like many studies in rural gerontology, findings of research in this area have been, however, somewhat contradictory. Lee and Cassidy concluded, for example, that the findings of their own and other studies "show generally small differences in the effects of widowhood according to residence" (1985, 156). But there is also evidence that the transition to widowhood may be exacerbated by location in a rural environment. Coward and Kerckhoff (as reported in Lassey et al. 1980) noted that elderly widows in rural areas may be more lonely and isolated because their children have moved from the region. In addition, they are often geographically isolated from health, recreation, and social services. For the rural widowed, lack of public transportation and physical distance from services create physical barriers to a social reconstruction of lifestyle in widowhood.

However, "one of the more enduring images of rural America is that of the family, self-reliant and caring for its own — especially the elderly." This image "has led to expectations of stronger, better integrated, and more extensive networks of familial support among the rural elderly" (Krout 1986, 124). Indeed, numerous researchers have suggested that indicators of greater isolation of the rural widowed are balanced by higher quality relationships with friends, family, and neighbours in the rural environment (Arling 1976; Fengler and Danigelis 1982; Roberto and Scott 1983). Harbert and Wilkinson (1979) reported that the elderly in rural areas have "informal neighbourhood support systems such as churches, friends and neighbours which are enviable in comparison to the apparent anonymity of some urban centres." On the basis of research on elderly women (most of them widowed) in a small Nova Scotia community, MacRae concluded that "a small relatively stable community does appear to offer advantages for identity management in old age, particularly in light of the availability of a sizeable number of age peers who have grown old together and who contribute to social integration" (1987, 397). In a study of 27 widows aged 60 and over, Cunningham (1988) found that those who chose to stay in a rural area after bereavement were typically long-time rural residents (mean average of 36 years) who dealt with the loss of the spouse in the supportive rural environment where they were born, reared, and lived most of their lives.

Research on the patterns of health care utilization and social support indicates that, where rural-urban differences exist, overall structural features of the rural environment, rather than characteristics of elders *per se*, account for the variability (Martin Matthews 1988b). Previous research on the rural aged concluded that, for the most part, the rural aged are as integrated as the urban into family and non-family support systems, and probably even more integrated (Martin Matthews 1988b). The reliability of these informal supports is, however, likely more precarious: children live farther away, the rural aged have fewer personal visits, they have older neighbours, and their access to formal supports is more limited. These factors likely explain their necessary reliance on the support of paid employees (Cape 1987).

The Ontario widowhood study included a rural-urban comparison of the social supports of the widowed, again measuring the three kinds of support as described previously. No statistically significant differences were found between the rural and the urban widowed on the measures of perceived support. Both groups indicated high levels of perceived support overall,

TABLE 4.3

PATTERNS OF SOCIAL SUPPORT IN WIDOWHOOD: RURAL-URBAN COMPARISONS

Measure	Rural Widowed $n = 86$		Urban Widowed $n = 66$	
	$\overline{X}$	s.d.	$\overline{X}$	s.d.
Numbers of Supporters				
Functional Children	1.8	1.3	1.8	1.4
Functional Siblings	0.8	1.2	0.7	0.9
Functional Relatives	0.8	1.2	1.0	1.4
Functional Friends	1.3	1.5	1.2	1.0
Total Functional Contacts	4.7	2.7	4.7	2.4
Face-to-Face Contacts				
Children	0.8	1.0	1.1	1.4
Siblings *	1.0*	1.7	0.6*	0.8
Other Relatives	0.8	1.4	1.1	1.5
Friends	0.8	1.2	0.6	0.8
Total	3.5	3.2	3.3	2.7
Telephone Contacts				
Children *	1.9*	1.8	1.1*	1.3
Siblings	1.1	1.4	1.2	1.5
Other Relatives	0.9	1.3	0.6	1.1
Friends	0.9	1.3	1.0	1.3
Total	4.8	3.1	3.9	2.9

* $p \leq .05$

and relatively high levels of perceived belonging, esteem, tangible, and appraisal support. Whatever their varying objective circumstances, both the rural and the urban widowed felt that significant support was available to them, across all dimensions.

Table 4.3 presents the findings with respect to patterns of social support in widowhood. Clearly, there were no significant differences between the rural and the urban widowed in the actual number of individuals available to them as functional members of their support networks. When we look at

TABLE 4.4

PREFERRED SOURCES OF SUPPORT IN WIDOWHOOD: RURAL-URBAN DIFFERENCES[a]

Situation Requiring Support		Self %	Child %	Sibling %	Friend/ Neighbour %	Other Relative %	Informal Org. %	Formal Org. %	Other %
Sick/dizzy at home	Rural	10.3	34.5	2.3	28.7	3.4	4.6	16.1	—
	Urban	9.4	40.6	9.4	18.8	3.1	4.7	14.1	—
Ride to doctor*	Rural	10.3	21.8	—	42.5	6.9	17.2	1.1	—
	Urban	6.3	31.3	4.7	15.6	6.3	32.8	3.1	—
Help after accident	Rural	—	9.4	2.4	2.4	4.7	1.2	80.0	—
	Urban	—	15.0	5.0	3.3	6.7	—	70.0	—
Change light bulb	Rural	48.2	8.2	—	18.8	11.8	11.8	1.2	—
	Urban	40.6	14.1	—	6.3	15.6	21.9	1.6	—
Fill out form	Rural	20.9	34.9	1.2	12.8	5.8	—	24.4	—
	Urban	24.6	30.8	—	7.7	15.4	—	21.5	—
Look after house	Rural	4.7	21.2	1.2	58.8	4.7	7.1	2.4	—
	Urban	1.6	31.1	3.3	49.2	6.6	4.9	3.3	—
Discuss family problem	Rural	9.4	21.2	8.2	27.1	20.0	—	12.9	1.2
	Urban	9.5	38.1	14.3	19.0	9.5	—	7.9	1.6
Advice/decision	Rural	11.5	39.1	2.3	13.8	9.2	—	23.0	1.1
	Urban	9.7	58.1	—	4.8	11.3	—	16.1	—
Companion for walk**	Rural	28.4	2.5	1.2	58.0	3.7	1.2	—	4.9
	Urban	40.7	6.8	3.4	39.0	6.8	—	3.4	—
Companion for shopping	Rural	13.3	16.9	4.8	51.8	10.8	—	2.4	—
	Urban	11.7	23.3	10.0	43.3	11.7	—	—	—
Company for holidays	Rural	1.1	34.5	1.1	26.4	36.8	—	—	—
	Urban	4.8	33.3	4.8	22.2	34.9	—	—	—
Feel worthwhile	Rural	7.1	14.1	2.4	45.9	18.8	2.4	9.4	—
	Urban	3.3	11.5	1.6	42.6	27.9	3.3	8.2	1.6

[a] Preferred sources indicated as first choice.
* *p* = .004
** *p* < .05

specific patterns of contact, different trends emerge. Among face-to-face contacts, the rural widowed had more siblings with whom they had direct personal contact than did the urban widowed. This finding is consistent with findings by Gibbs (1985), who compared patterns of social interaction of the widowed in rural and urban Kansas. She reported more personal contact with siblings by the rural widowed, although there were no rural-urban differences in felt closeness to siblings (Gibbs 1985).

For telephone contacts, a similar pattern emerges, again showing that the rural widowed had slightly more contact with support network members. Rural widows and widowers had significantly more telephone contact with adult children than did their urban counterparts. Again, this finding is consistent with that reported by Gibbs (1985) in the U.S., although she noted that the urban widowed correspond by letter more with children. The significant differences in patterns of telephone contact with children become particularly intriguing in the light of the finding that "feelings of emotional closeness are not contingent on quantities of specific social interaction, except for talking on the telephone" (Gibbs 1985, 97).

Table 4.4 presents the findings concerning preferred sources of support, that is, those individuals on whom the widowed would call for certain specific types of assistance. The table illustrates the percentages of elderly widowed people who would turn to various family members, friends/ neighbours, formal organizations, or to self/no one for assistance. These data indicate that, with the exception of emergency circumstances relating to an accident, the widowed rural elderly typically sought the assistance of informal supports, and most particularly family members, in the twelve situations examined. This supports the findings of other rural research that "informal supports were relied upon to the exclusion of formal supports...when the respondent was widowed" (Scott and Roberto 1985, 629). In addition, family members other than children were not typically the choice for support in most situations. Siblings, for example (despite their frequency of personal contact with the widowed), were infrequently chosen as a source of support, confirming the findings of Lopata (1978; 1979) that siblings are not a substantial source of exchanged aid or tangible support. This is consistent for both the rural and the urban widowed.

The data in Table 4.4 indicate only two help-seeking situations where the rural and the urban widowed elderly differed significantly in their preferred choice of support. For assistance relating to tangible support in obtaining transportation to visit a physician, the rural widowed elderly were most likely to ask help of a neighbour or a friend, while the urban widowed chose to seek help from a child or such organizational supports as a taxi service or a seniors' group. Also, in terms of seeking companionship for a walk, the rural widowed were less likely to go alone, and more likely to choose the company of a neighbour or a friend, than were their urban counterparts.

Other analyses of these data on the rural and the urban widowed used four different measures of rurality in order more extensively to examine differences between the rural and the urban widowed. On the basis of repeated calls in the literature for more precision in the conceptualization and measurement of rurality, four measures of urban and rural were used: current residence; duration (at least 15 years) in community of residence; residence at age 16; and a self-definition as rural or urban (Martin Matthews 1988b). More rural-urban differences emerged when the residence at age 16 measure was used than for any of the measures involving current residence or self-definition. Using this measure, significant differences emerged in the assessment of belonging support, tangible support, and total telephone contact with the support network: those who were rural at age 16 perceived more such support and had significantly more telephone contact than those urban at age 16.

Overall, the Ontario widowhood data show that there are many more similarities than differences between the rural and the urban widowed. Where differences existed, the rural widowed reported more face-to-face contact with siblings, more telephone contact with support network members overall and with children in particular. What emerges is a picture of rural widowed persons as having somewhat more supports. Not only is current rural residence associated with more support; having been a rural resident or defining oneself as rural is also associated with greater supports in widowhood. Evidently, widowed elders who grew up in rural areas or who define themselves as rural receive more of certain kinds of support, and are more likely to report being satisfied with the levels of support they do receive.

However, in the Ontario widowhood study, the widowed who resided in rural areas had lower socio-economic status and had been widowed for shorter lengths of time. The average length of widowhood among the rural sample was 8.9 years, compared to 12.9 years among the urban respondents. There is the possibility that *these* differences, rather than location in a rural environment, might account for observed differences in support patterns. When the effect of socio-economic status on the relationship between present residence and patterns of personal contact with siblings is statistically controlled, the relationship no longer holds. However, when the effect of length of widowhood is statistically controlled, a significant relationship between rural residence and patterns of face-to-face contact with siblings is still obtained. The relationship between rural residence and patterns of telephone contact with children remains significant when the effect of socio-economic status is held constant, and when length of widowhood is statistically controlled.

Overall, these data show that the rural widowed, in terms of their own perception of available social supports, patterns of support, and sources of support, are by no means disadvantaged. Despite the frequent general perception that adult children are often more distant and rural elders may experience greater social isolation, these findings suggest that this is not the case in this sample.

The rural widowed in this study did receive somewhat more support than did their urban counterparts, especially in terms of telephone contacts. Nevertheless, they did not translate this greater actual support into a perception that supports were more readily available. One must therefore concur with Lee and Cassidy (1985, 165) that rural families do not "possess any unique strengths which ameliorate the effects of other privations upon their family members."

Despite the finding that the rural widowed have only somewhat more support than do the urban widowed, the perception existed among the participants in the Ontario widowhood study that living in a rural area is an advantage in widowhood. Fully 56 percent felt this way, compared with 33 percent who favoured the urban environment, 5 percent who felt there was no difference, and another 5 percent unable to answer. The responses were given to the question of whether "living in a village or small town is an advantage or disadvantage compared to living in a city when you are your age and widowed." They revealed a strong perception of rural areas as "warmer" and more tightly knit social environments.

> I think the small town would be an advantage because everyone knows everyone. You'd have more close friends, really. I know practically everyone in these two buildings, but they are acquaintances. [Currently urban]

> There is an advantage in the rural area. You know more people. In the city, however, shopping is easier, transportation is easier. Actually, the city has more advantages other than knowing people. [Currently urban]

Most intriguing is the finding that urban residents were far more likely than the rural widowed to feel this way.

HOUSING: COMMUNITY AND INSTITUTION

The Community

As discussed in Chapter 1, differential rates in the likelihood of being widowed have significant implications for the living arrangements of men and women in old age. The majority of older men live in families with a spouse or their never-married children. Partly because of their pattern of earlier widowhood, the proportion of elderly women in such family settings decreases dramatically as they age. They increasingly live in non-family households, either alone in "private households" (36 percent of women aged 75 and over) or as residents of collective dwellings (20 percent of women aged 75 and over). But once age 80 is reached, the proportion of women living alone declines sharply, with an increasing proportion living in collective dwellings. It is important to note that the large proportion of older women living alone is a relatively new phenomenon in Canada. Between 1961 and 1981, the proportion of women aged 65 and over living alone doubled from 16 percent to 32 percent (Health and Welfare Canada 1983). Greater economic security in old age, acquired through the introduction of public pension plans (C/QPP) and income supplements (GIS), and the development of more community-based health and social service programs, are credited with enabling the elderly to live independently for longer than was previously possible.

Almost two-thirds (62 percent) of a sample of Australian widowed lived alone, and 5 percent lived with siblings (McCallum 1986). In Canadian studies of widowed women, as many as 73 percent of the widowed lived alone (Martin Matthews 1982). In Stryckman's research in Quebec, only 23 percent of the widowed were living alone, but fully one-third (32 percent) were living in quasi-family settings, typically with a sister or a female friend. Such an arrangement was described as bringing satisfaction to the

TABLE **4.5**

LIVING ARRANGEMENT PATTERNS AND HISTORIES:
MARITAL STATUS COMPARISONS

Variable	Widowed *n* = 152	Separated/Divorced *n* = 19	Never Married *n* = 62
	%	%	%
Duration of Community Residence*			
16 - 20 years	17.2	10.5	4.8
20 + years	50.3	26.3	69.4
Whole life	7.3	10.5	9.7
Duration of Current Residence*			
11 - 15 years	11.3	15.8	16.1
16 - 20 years	17.3	10.5	9.7
20 + years	25.3	10.5	35.5
Type of Residence			
Single Family Dwelling	54.3	42.1	61.3
Apartment	36.4	47.4	30.6
Tenancy			
Ownership	58.3	42.1	60.7
Live Alone	79.6	84.2	79.0

* $p \leq .05$

SOURCE: Martin Matthews.

widowed in terms of needing someone to take care of them (Stryckman 1982, 144-45). These figures are rather different from those reported in Ontario, and may reflect francophone/anglophone differences in living arrangements in later life. Co-residence with adult children is not typical among the widowed in any studies. An analysis of U.S. national data found that the likelihood of co-residence with offspring is greatest for women who become widowed in middle age, when women turn to adult children for residential help to assist them in coping with an off-time event (Cooney 1989).

Table 4.5 summarizes data on the living arrangement patterns and histories of individuals in the Ontario widowhood study. It also introduces marital status comparisons between the widowed, separated/divorced, and never married, comparisons to be explored more fully in Chapter 5. These data indicate that the continuity of the residential location, both in terms of the community of residence and the particular housing unit, was striking. The vast majority of the widowed had lived at least 20 years in the same community. Indeed, approximately 43 percent of the widowed had been in the same accommodation for 16 or more years.

These findings are consistent with the very limited body of literature on marital status comparisons of mobility status among older women. Unlike divorce, which may occasion relocation, the transition to widowhood is not necessarily associated with relocation. In the early years of bereavement, there may even be pressures to delay relocation because of the "stabilizing force" (Hartwigsen 1987) that the family home represents in a time of emotional upheaval. Overall, the available data suggest that widows are not particularly inclined to relocate after their husband's death (O'Bryant 1987) and may indeed derive comfort in the many memories and associations of the conjugal home (Bowling and Cartwright 1982). Lopata (1979) found that after an average of 11 years of widowhood, over half the women in her Chicago sample lived in the same housing units. The average length of residence in their present home was 26 years among a sample of Ohio widows (McGloshen and O'Bryant 1988).

The significance attached to the issue of home ownership among widowed women is, however, a controversial issue. The data in the Ontario widowhood study indicate that high proportions of widowed women have ownership of single family dwellings. While this may inherently be a good thing, home ownership may not necessarily signify economic security for older women. In the United States, the median value of the houses owned by older women living alone has been calculated at fully 28 percent less than the median value of all owner-occupied houses (O'Bryant 1987). Moreover, widowed women must "maintain their homes on an income much lower in proportion to the value of their homes than is the case of other elderly homeowners" (O'Bryant 1987, 52). In addition, concomitant with the drop in income typically associated with widowhood, such housing-related expenses as mortgage payments (if any), utility costs, maintenance, insurance, and repairs remain constant or increase (O'Bryant 1982). Home ownership may in fact be as much of a disadvantage as an advantage for the low-income unattached woman.

The long residential tenure of the widowed population studied in Ontario should not be taken to indicate that widowhood is necessarily associated with residential stability. Research on the rural elderly in particular suggests that non-institutional relocation is associated with the death of the spouse (Colsher and Wallace 1990). Similar conclusions have been drawn about other widowed populations (Rogers 1988; Kendig 1990). It is typically the case that "marital status shifts...often trigger living arrangement passages" (Stone and Fletcher 1987, 306). Because "the passage from one living arrangement to another is not only sometimes a stressful process for those involved [and] may also reduce access to....informal helping networks" (ibid., 291), the widowed may in fact be more disadvantaged than the long-term single in this regard.

The issue of relocation is highly salient for widowed individuals, even if they do in fact remain residentially stable. While there is substantial debate in the gerontological literature about the impact of relocation on morbidity and mortality, particularly among frail elderly populations and those living in institutionalized settings, there is no doubt that the timing of relocation decisions presents a particular quandary for the widowed. As two women in the Ontario widowhood study indicated:

> A lot of us must deal with the prospect of going into some sort of nursing care facility when we become unable to look after ourselves. The big problem is— do you go somewhere to be close to your family or do you stay close to your friends? Family must be free to move themselves, whenever the need arises and the other aspect to keep in mind is that friends are slowly but surely dying off. It becomes a very hard decision to make since you don't want to end up totally alone. [73-year-old woman, widowed 6 years]

> I have to make a decision as to whether I should sell the house and go into an apartment. I don't want to be a burden to my friends or family....It's just to make the move. I've moved around so much; I just want to make one last move. It's a debate as to whether to stay with friends or move to be close to family. [74-year-old woman, widowed 7 years]

Among the widowed, the factors contributing to a decision to relocate include having fewer relatives in the neighbourhood (O'Bryant and Murray 1986), and increased frailty (Longino 1990).

Most of the widowed in the Ontario study who expressed any regrets at all about major changes or decisions that they had made in their lives had regrets in terms of housing.

> I wish now that I hadn't been so quick to sell my house. If I had been able to get someone to come live with me I might have been able to be independent a little longer. [Woman aged 91, widowed 10 years]

Moving...brought me face to face with the reality that life doesn't go on as before. You have to make some adjustments. [Woman aged 69, widowed 2 years]

Clearly, there are challenges in examining the issue of appropriate housing for the widowed. The widows in the Ontario study were rather remarkably stable in their residential settings, as were those studied in Winnipeg (Harvey and Harris 1985), in New Brunswick (Arsenault 1986), in rural Nova Scotia (MacRae 1987), and in the United States. Older widows are very long-term residents of their communities and quite long-term residents of their current homes and apartments. This stability may occur because of many socio-emotional reasons of attachment to home (O'Bryant 1987; Gnaedinger 1986), and because of the importance of the continuity of personal possessions (McCracken 1988). But the question remains whether residential stability, particularly in single family dwellings, is the most appropriate to the needs of older widowed women. The mutually supportive environments of seniors' apartment buildings, for example, provide an alternative context in which many widowed women age successfully (Elias 1977). For many widowed women, residential stability often means remaining in a house that is no longer appropriate to one's needs and in a neighbourhood that has changed in profile and purpose. Such stability may be the price that widows pay in order to achieve and maintain a measure of economic self-sufficiency. The single family dwelling, inappropriate as it may be otherwise, is paid for and enables the widow to live without worries of rent increases and without anxieties that one will live longer than one's assets. Alternatives may also be unavailable. In small communities, in which widowed women are concentrated, subsidized seniors' apartments may be few and vacancies rare. Thus, either because alternatives are simply not available or because they are too costly, widows frequently remain in their own homes, because doing so gives them "peace of mind."

Institutionalization

In terms of the living arrangements of Canada's aged, the popular image is that most of the elderly live in institutions. However, in 1981, only 9 percent of the older population lived in collective dwellings (Health and Welfare Canada 1983, 68). The proportion of aged who are in institutional settings varies widely from province to province, from a low of about 5.6 percent in Newfoundland, to 9.1 percent in Ontario, to 9.4 percent in Alberta (Schwenger and Gross 1980, 251).

In spite of the evidence from the cross-sectional data that comparatively small proportions of the aged live in institutional settings at any given time, it has been estimated that approximately 25 percent of the aged will spend at least some portion of their later years in an institutional setting (Vincente et al. 1979). There is also clear evidence that being widowed in later life substantially increases the risk of institutionalization. Data compiled on the institutionalized population consistently indicate that the widowed are overrepresented proportionally among the ranks of the elderly who must seek institutional care in later life (Forbes et al. 1987, 42). Indeed, Kraus (1976) found that living with a spouse was much less frequent among applicants to institutions than among the elderly living in the community who had not applied for admission to an institution (19 percent vs. 56 percent), while living alone was somewhat more frequent among the applicants to institutions (35 percent vs. 26 percent) (Forbes et al. 1987, 41).

PARENTAL STATUS

The issue of the extent to which the presence of adult children in any way buffers the impact of widowhood in later life has been examined in a number of contexts. These discussions recall the analysis in Chapter 3 of the assumptions that family support is inherently beneficial and supportive. It is important to acknowledge that approximately 15 percent of the ever-married female population aged 65 and over are childless (Statistics Canada 1983). One would expect the childless widowed to have rather different support networks than do widowed parents.

One of the primary methods for examining this issue in the gerontological literature is through the comparison of widowed individuals who have children and those who are childless. In Great Britain, researchers Bowling and Cartwright (1982) found essentially no difference between the childless elderly and those with children in terms of their overall adjustment to bereavement. While Rempel (1985) similarly found no significant difference between the elderly with or without children on a variety of quality of life measures such as satisfaction and loneliness, Stryckman found that widows who have children judge their previous marriage more negatively than do the childless. There was also evidence that the childless widowed had developed significant networks of social relations to compensate for childlessness, especially with nieces, nephews, and siblings (Stryckman 1981a; Lopata 1979). While the Ontario widowhood study contained too few childless widowed to make statistical comparisons, these individuals did appear extensively involved in networks of other kin and did not appear any less socially engaged than did widowed parents.

Although the childless widowed may not be disadvantaged in patterns of access to social supports, other problems of widowhood may be associated with childlessness. A study of 120 women widowed from one month to 5 years, with a mean age of 63 years, 17 of whom were childless, found that "the childless group showed depression scores significantly higher than the group with children" (Smith 1978). Age served as a mitigating factor here, however. Younger widows with children were often very depressed because of the devastating sense of having more responsibility than they could manage. Among the later-life widowed, childlessness was associated with higher levels of depression, while among the younger widowed, the reverse was true.

Because of the prevalence of adult children in the social support networks of the widowed, the literature has largely assumed that the childless widowed are a particularly disadvantaged group. This does not, however, appear to be the case.

ETHNICITY AND CULTURE

The issue of the extent to which identification with a particular minority ethnic group complicates the process of adaptation to widowhood in later life has not been systematically investigated in Canada. Lopata was among the first to empirically examine the correlates of minority group identification among widows, and she observed distinctive ethnic differences in living arrangement patterns. For example, while 78 percent of British and Italian widows lived alone, none of the Greek widows did; they all lived with married children, in accordance with cultural practice. Just as Vachon, Rogers, et al. (1982) found in their bereavement studies in Toronto, there were substantial ethnic differences in the extent to which widows were involved in the mother role, with Irish, Polish, and Italian widows strongly involved and Germans substantially less so (Lopata 1973b). By and large, however, available data do not support the popular assumption of more extended networks, and more involvement in those networks, by ethnic widows and widowers (Driedger and Chappell 1987, 69). Indeed, Australian data suggest that widowed individuals "at greatest 'ethnic distance' from the mainstream" experience more psychological distress. "This result further gives credence to the argument...that ethnic enclaves may be less effective in old age for buffering stress" (McCallum and Shadbolt 1989, S95).

In a study of 26 elderly Chinese women widowed between three and ten years and living in rooming houses in Montreal's Chinatown, Chan found that, far from increasing the dependency of these women on their families because of widowhood, "the death of their husbands seemed to have intensified their desire to move out on their own, preferably in areas with a substantial Chinese population" (1983, 45). While women who ascribe to the traditional widow role (Vachon, Rogers, et al. 1982) immerse themselves in kin ties following bereavement, the widows described by Chan did the opposite, immersing themselves in their culture but reducing their dependency on family and the family's second-generation norms and values. This phenomenon recalls Lopata's statement of the potential opportunity for growth that widowhood may afford some women:

What may be happening, although there are not many indications as yet of an overwhelming trend, is that women freed from the controls of the family institution through widowhood may be purposely disrupting the vestiges of their prior role clusters after the "grief work" is done and entering roles and lifestyles that they never would have considered in girlhood and wifehood, becoming independent functioning units rather than being dependent upon passive acceptance of membership in units dominated by others (Lopata 1975, 233).

While Lopata was not referring specifically to the ethnic widowed, this observation appears particularly appropriate in the light of the adaptations of the Chinese widowed as described by Chan.

While the experience of widowhood may vary for members of ethnic groups living within a predominantly Anglo-Saxon culture, broad cultural differences also characterize widowhood in an international perspective. As Harvey and Bahr (1980, 139) have noted, international studies have established that widowhood is quite differently perceived around the world. Among the better known cultural practices are the Indian custom of suttee, in which the widow immolates herself on her husband's funeral pyre, and the levirate custom whereby the widow automatically marries one of her husband's kin. Lopata's (1987a) edited volume on widowhood in the Middle East, Asia, and the Pacific represents a pioneering effort to advance the understanding of the role of widow outside Western culture.

FINANCIAL RESOURCES

A focus on the financial resources of the widowed elderly raises the issue not only of the socio-economic status of this population, but also of recent trends in social policy with respect to the aged in general and the widowed in particular. In this discussion, it is important to note Morgan's (1981) finding that estimates of economic well-being among the widowed, as for all marital status groups, vary considerably depending on the selected measure. Total household income, per capita income, and poverty-based income each provide different information about an individual's economic security. Time intervals selected for measures of change in income may also influence the research findings. David and Fitzgerald (1988), for example, have suggested that measuring poverty over a short period will enlarge the count of poor by adding to the chronically poor a group that has temporary hardships. They have also argued that the deprivation of the aged tends to be overstated by income measures as compared with consumption patterns, citing specifically the example of elderly widows who have relatively low incomes but "sizeable quantities of liquid assets" (David and Fitzgerald 1988, 19). With these caveats in mind, and recognizing that studies do not always use comparable measures, let us now consider the financial resources of the elderly widowed.

There are several ways of doing this: by examining the financial status of elderly people who are widowed; by comparing the financial status of the widowed with that of elderly members of other marital status groups; and by analyzing changes in financial status accompanying the transition to widowhood. Each of these is considered in the following section.

The examination of the financial status of the widowed elderly reveals that "the high frequency of poverty among widows when poverty is defined by income is also found when poverty is defined by wealth" (Hurd and Wise 1987, 31). There is a significant relationship between being widowed and experiencing serious financial problems (Arens 1982). Despite some notable reductions in levels of poverty among Canada's elderly during the past decade, those who are "unattached" (either because they never married, or were separated, divorced, or widowed) "still run a very high likelihood of being poor (42.7 percent in 1986)..." (National Council of Welfare 1988). Poverty is defined as the spending of approximately 58.5 percent of one's income for food, clothing, and shelter. Unattached women are particularly vulnerable. Almost half (46.1 percent) of unattached elderly women, most of them widows, are poor compared to 31.9 percent of unattached men aged 65 and over (National Council of Welfare 1988). Although these figures are high, they do indicate some substantial improvement in the risk of poverty among the aged, and among the widowed in particular. In 1982, the comparable rates of poverty among the unattached elderly were 60.4 percent for women and 48.9 percent for men (National Council of Welfare 1984). These improvements in the overall financial situation of the elderly likely reflect some recent increments in the Guaranteed Income Supplement, and the fact that those retiring today have increased access to better pensions than did those who retired a decade ago (National Council of Welfare 1988). Nevertheless, it is clear that widowhood in later life is frequently associated with falling below the low-income cut-off. As will be discussed in Chapter 6, various policy initiatives have been undertaken in Canada to address the issue of the economic insecurity of specific groups of widowed individuals.

These problems also exist in the U.S., where Clark (1990, 384) has noted that, despite the improved economic status of the elderly in recent decades, widowed women still "face severe economic problems." It is estimated that one-half of all widows in the United States live at or below the income adequacy level determined by the Social Security Administration (Balkwell 1981) and that, among the retired, elderly widows are the only group who actually "dissave" either by borrowing money or by using previously acquired assets (Hurd 1987). Although there is some evidence that gender is not an important predictor of poverty among the widowed (Smith and Zick 1986), the findings of a U.S. longitudinal study indicate that widowed women experience a substantially higher risk of poverty than do widowers (Holden et al. 1986).

An analysis of data from the U.S. National Longitudinal Surveys cohort of mature women found that 40 percent of widows and over one-quarter of divorced women experience poverty for at least some time during the first five years after the end of a marriage (Morgan 1989). However, on different measures, including a full range of economic well-being scores rather than just the low-end cut-off of the poverty level, Morgan found no marital status differences among unmarried women. For widowed and divorced women, "the mean income index scores for both groups decreased over time, suggesting an erosion of the income position of these women relative to where they stood during marriage" (Morgan 1989, 98). Data from the Ontario widowhood study indicate significant differences between marital status groups on measures of household income. The never married had higher income levels than the widowed, who in turn had higher levels of income than did the separated/divorced. Data from the U.S. Census and Current Population survey show the widowed and long-term divorced women to have significantly lower levels of financial well-being than married women (Uhlenberg et al. 1990).

For many of the widowed, the experience of bereavement precipitates relative poverty among individuals who had not been poor as a member of a couple (Hurd and Wise 1987). Hudson (1984) found that most widows are worse off financially two years after widowhood than before, and that the drop in total family income begins in the year *before* widowhood, when the ill spouse is no longer able to continue working or high health care costs deplete income. Most of the Chicago widows studied by Lopata (1979) experienced a large drop in income between the year before widowhood and the time of the study. Indeed, an analysis of data from the U.S. Panel Study of Income Dynamics found that, after five years, fully 33 percent of an initially non-poor sample of widows and widowers had experienced at least one year of poverty (Smith and Zick 1986, 629). There was some evidence that "longer marriages serve to insulate survivors from extreme poverty," possibly because these partners simply had had more time to acquire economic resources (ibid.).

Nevertheless, not *all* widowed individuals experience the transition to poverty. A sample of German widows participating in the Bonn Longitudinal Study of Aging experienced considerable improvement in their financial circumstances during the 12 years of the study (Fooken 1985). In terms of economic well-being, less than half of a U.S. sample of widowed women reported that their economic circumstances had declined since the loss of their husbands, and only one in five felt that their current status left them with problems in getting along on their current income (O'Bryant and Morgan 1989). Some of these widowed were, however, of an age where they received Social Security benefits. There is in the literature a recognition of the "widow's gap which befalls nonworking women who no longer have dependent children and have not yet reached [pensionable age]" (Morgan 1987, 689). The relationship between the age at which widowhood is experienced and the likelihood of poverty has also been demonstrated by Smith and Zick. They found that "those widowed between the ages of 50 and 62 are almost twelve times more likely to fall into poverty than are those widowed prior to age 50" (1986, 623). They concluded that "those widowed in their 50s are quite adversely affected" (1986, 625).

The issue of the financial resources available to a widowed person is important not only as a source of variability among the widowed. It also has significance in relation to the process of adaptation to widowhood in later life. Both in economic terms and in social-psychological terms, the impact of lack of financial resources is apparent. "Poverty impoverishes all of life including the emotional level" (Lopata 1979, 345), with poor widows having fewer emotional supports than do the non-poor. Differences in morale between widows and married women disappeared when the effects of income were statistically controlled (Morgan 1976), although Harvey et al. (1987) noted a lesser importance of income as a predictor of morale in Canadian data as compared with U.S. data on widowed persons. Nevertheless, among the widowed in the Ontario study, financial concerns loomed large in descriptions of the problems associated with widowhood in later life.

> I'm worried about major expenses such as the need for a new roof (which needs doing), the cost of a car and perhaps a new furnace. That's quite a major outlay for me to have to make and my resources are not that great. [Woman aged 90, widowed 13 years]
>
> I always seem to be worried about finances. There isn't enough pension money for a single person. House upkeep is the same, even though there is only one of you now. [Woman aged 65, widowed 3 years]
>
> Financial. Have I saved enough to get by on? [Man aged 64, widowed 2 years]

Other studies have similarly found that financial concerns are a major problem for the widowed, particularly women (Lopata 1973b; Stryckman 1982).

So important is income to the understanding of widowhood in later life that "the negative impact sometimes attributed to widowhood derives not from the widowhood status, but rather from socioeconomic status" (Harvey and Bahr 1974, 104). Other researchers concur that much of the negative impact of conjugal bereavement is more directly correlated with change in income than change in marital status, although Lehman et al. (1987) found that most differences between bereaved spouses and controls were greater than would have been expected on the basis of differences in present family income.

Regardless of the degree of change in financial resources accompanying widowhood, the economic realities and financial tasks associated with the loss of one's spouse in later life may be quite daunting. These economic realities, as noted by Morgan (1981), may include the costs of the spouse's illness and death, legal settlement of the estate, and adaptation to a new status as a single-income household. The widowed may face the dire necessity of having to improve their financial status, possibly having to learn how to earn an income (Morgan 1981). These activities may well occur with little or no prior planning, for as Morgan (1986) indicates, only 43 percent of wives have discussed with their husbands issues involving financial planning for the future.

CONCLUSION

The experience of widowhood in later life is associated with a very heterogeneous population whose involvement in social supports is highly variable. This chapter examined several of the socio-demographic factors that contribute both to the diversity of the widowed population, and to the social supports available to them and the networks in which they engage.

Many factors distinguish the experience of widowhood for men and for women. The greater expectability of widowhood as a life course event for women frequently leads to a mental rehearsal or anticipation of circumstances associated with being "unattached" in later life. Although considerable research has debated whether the loss of the spouse is more difficult for men than for women, the findings are equivocal. The challenge of addressing these comparisons with appropriate scientific rigour is complicated by the demography of widowhood, where studies of the widowed often result in samples that are only about 13 percent males. Despite these research difficulties, studies have identified differences between widows and widowers in attitudes towards remarriage and in the issues that are most problematic to them in widowhood. Loneliness is a major problem for both genders; financial resources are a concern for widows; and completion of household tasks and sexuality issues are major areas of concern for widowers. On measures of social support focusing on sources, patterns, and perceptions of support, there are also gender differences. The widowers had smaller support networks and overall less involvement with support network members that did widows. In accessing support, widowers relied almost exclusively on themselves or their children. Widows by contrast had much more extensive and diverse networks, and relied on different kinds of supporters for different kinds of tasks, depending on their availability. Despite the finding of the greater vulnerability of the widowers in patterns of access to social supports, men were in fact much less likely than women to believe that widowhood is more difficult for males.

Comparisons of the rural and urban widowed showed that overall there are many more similarities than differences between the two. Where differences do exist, they show the widowed residing in rural areas to have somewhat more supports, especially in terms of telephone contacts. Even having been a rural resident in the past or defining oneself as rural is associated with more supports in widowhood. While there was no compelling evidence for substantially greater involvement in social support among the rural elderly, the perception remains that living in a rural area is an advantage in widowhood.

An increasing number of widowed persons in Canada live alone, many of them residing in the same community and the same housing unit for 16 or more years. Although home ownership may be an important source of economic security for the widowed, high housing-related costs may seriously undermine the financial benefits of ownership. In addition, long residential tenure, often for reasons of sentimental attachment to home as well as inertia at the prospect of relocation, may confine the widowed to a home whose physical characteristics are no longer appropriate to their needs and to a neighbourhood no longer able to provide a supportive environment. When relocation finally comes for those widowed in later life, it is often into an institutional setting. Although less than 10 percent of aged Canadians are institutionalized, the widowed are proportionally overrepresented among those who seek institutional care in later life.

Other factors that contribute to the variability of widowhood include whether or not the widowed have living children, and ethnic identification and culture. Childlessness does not appear to exacerbate the transition to widowhood. There also appears to be little empirical support for the popular assumption of more extended networks and more involvement in those networks by widows and widowers with strong ethnic group identification.

The experience of widowhood also varies in terms of the financial resources available to the widowed. Not all widowed persons are poor, and widowers are certainly less likely to be poor than are widows. While rates of poverty have been reduced among elderly widowed women in Canada in the past decade, a drop in income is typically associated with widowhood, and many widowed persons are very likely to experience poverty in later life. For many of these, the experience of bereavement precipitates poverty among individuals who had not been poor as a member of a couple. Financial concerns loom large among the problems associated with widowhood.

While all of these factors contribute to the heterogeneity of the experience of widowhood in later life, there are many ways in which the social worlds of the widowed are quite distinct from those of other individuals who are "unattached" in later life. Through comparisons with other marital status groups, Chapter 5 examines selected factors that are unique to the experience of widowhood in old age.

CHAPTER 5

BEING SINGLE IN LATER LIFE: MARITAL STATUS COMPARISONS AND COMPETING ROLE DEMANDS

INTRODUCTION

Chapter 4 considered factors that contribute to an understanding of the heterogeneity of widowhood. In this chapter the focus is on the unique features of the experience of widowhood in later life, through a comparison of widowhood with other marital statuses and life course transitions.

Most studies of the widowed do not include control groups of those who have not experienced bereavement, or of those who have experienced other kinds of losses. As a result,

> In the absence of a control group..., conclusions that the patterns observed are effects of widowhood may be false. At best, the investigator has...a *pseudocomparative* research design, one in which he uses his imagination or general fund of knowledge to fill in the findings for the cell that is in fact missing in the design. If he had a truly comparative design, he might learn that his imagination had led him astray. [Hyman 1983, 9]

In studies that use comparative designs, the most typical control group is the married, although both the widowed and the married represent "selected, relatively healthy groups of survivors" (Hyman 1983, 15) — both survived marriage. A more appropriate control group for use in isolating the distinctive effects of widowhood is the separated or divorced, who also have "lost or relinquished a spouse, although less irrevocably than the widowed and for reasons that are varied and sometimes welcome but surely different" (Hyman 1983, 17). The Ontario widowhood study was part of a larger panel study that also included data on a sample of separated/ divorced individuals, and a sample of never-married elders. When these marital status groups are compared on selected dimensions of social support and well-being, the pitfalls of the pseudocomparative design are avoided, "and a truly comparative design containing two control groups" is utilized (Hyman 1983, 17).

WIDOWHOOD VERSUS SEPARATION AND DIVORCE

The study of life course transitions usually involves the examination of such "typical" life events as getting married, having children, the departure of children from the home, retiring from the paid labour force, and becoming a widow or widower. Because most events of this sort are linked to the family life cycle, a characteristic feature is their general predictability. Although there is some variation in the timing of life-cycle transitions, they can be viewed as the relatively scheduled and anticipated events of life (Pearlin 1980). Widowhood is such a life event, and it differs fundamentally from other life-cycle events like divorce and illness, which may be widely experienced but nevertheless are "not scheduled into our lives as we do the life-cycle transitions" (Pearlin 1980, 351).

While this volume attests to the now well-established tradition of research on many facets of the transition to widowhood, it continues to be the case that "little is known about the effects on individuals of becoming divorced in later life or living as a divorced elderly person" (Hennon 1983, 149). Troll et al. observed ten years ago that "divorce is one of the most neglected areas of gerontological research" (1979, 80), and their statement remains true today. What little we do know suggests that there are indeed some differences in the adaptations involved in the *process* of becoming a divorced versus a widowed person in later life.

Both widowhood and divorce are conditions under which formerly married people become, and may remain, single in later life. However, the consequences of divorce may be more severe or different for several reasons. Widowhood is a more institutionalized status, more "normal" and expectable in our society. Also, with death, the spouse is only psychologically present to effect self-concept, while with divorce he or she can be both psychologically and physically present. The entire social-psychological definition of becoming unmarried differs for each transition. As discussed previously, widowed persons often "sanctify the memory" of the deceased spouse (Lopata 1979), while the divorced may experience quite different feelings of anger, guilt, and frustration. Many of the emotional responses found to be common to the divorced, such as shame, guilt, hurt, or rejection, are usually not found among the widowed (O'Bryant and Straw 1991). In contrast, the widowed may have more problems with feelings of dependency (Lund 1989a). The impact of divorce will also vary as a function of whether or not it was desired. Hennon, for example, has noted the differences between a woman who desires divorce due to perceived incompetence in her husband and a woman who is "dumped" for a younger woman. In addition, divorce may occasion a sense of failure after many years of marriage (Hennon 1983), and this may complicate the process of adaptation.

Overall, widowhood, in comparison with divorce, has better-established norms and self-expectations for behaviour, as well as uniformity in the expectations of others (Hennon 1983). This provides a form of social support that is lacking for the divorced person. There is some evidence (Gove 1973, 1979, 1982; Gove and Shin 1989) that there are more physical and mental health problems among the divorced than among the widowed.

In one of the few empirical investigations of the experience of divorce in later life, Hennon utilized data from 40 individuals (20 each of divorced and widowed women), with the divorced and widowed matched by age, rural/urban residence, and length of time single since the termination of the marriage. In comparisons of these groups, who each had a mean age of 69, and who had been single after marriage for an average of approximately 20 years, the widowed fared better than the divorced in that they had higher incomes, were more satisfied with their financial situations, had fewer money worries, were more religious, and were more integrated into kin support networks (Hennon 1983, 168). Characteristics common to both groups included loneliness, concerns about children, fear of becoming dependent and of declining health, and a sense of powerlessness. Overall, these data suggest that "divorced elderly women, as a group, are not worse off, except financially and perhaps kin system-wise, than widowed elderly women" (Hennon 1983, 171).

Other studies confirm the greater psychological deprivation felt by the divorced. Older divorced women feel much worse off than do widows not only in relation to financial matters but also in terms of self-esteem and relations with others (Troll et al. 1979; Uhlenberg and Myers 1981). Another factor that may distinguish later-life divorce and widowhood in social-psychological terms is the issue of stigma. While "widowhood is more likely to be seen as a sad experience, divorce is considered as a sinful or shameful one" (Troll et al. 1979, 80). Because of the social stigma that may be attached to the divorced status among the aged population in particular, there may well be underreporting of being divorced among the elderly (Uhlenberg and Myers 1981).

Findings from age-standardized survey data, which focused primarily on women, concluded that the greater clarity of the widowed role may provide more social support and ease adjustment to the end of a marriage for the widow in ways unavailable to the divorcee, whose status is still stigmatized. "Although widows and divorcees claim indignantly that they have little in common, a number of observers report that the bereavement process through which each moves has several similar characteristics" (Kitson et al. 1980, 292). But there are also important differences. Major changes in life and social status have wide-ranging social consequences for the person involved, and these consequences differ for divorced and widowed women. "In every case the divorcees' attitudes reflect a greater sense of restriction and isolation from others than do the widows." In particular, "divorcees...feel that relatives are their only true friends" (Kitson et al. 1980, 295-97).

Kitson et al. report some noteworthy findings concerning the age-related experience of widowhood and divorce. When differences in the age of the divorcees and the widows were controlled for, widows felt less restricted in their relationships with others than did the divorcees. Nevertheless, each transition had its own disadvantages. Adjustment to the loss of a spouse may be made more difficult by the fact that women generally are older when their husbands die, and widows may therefore also face age discrimination. In contrast, divorced women experience discrimination and report a sense of alienation and restriction in relationships with others "that is *based on their divorced status*" (Kitson et al. 1980, 299). This leads to the conclusion that "...if a widow and a divorcee were of the same age, we might expect that the divorcee, because of her sense of restricted relationships with others, would seek and receive less support from them. This suggests that the divorcee's adjustment to her new status might be even more difficult than that of the widow, since social supports do ease adjustment to divorce and widowhood" (Kitson et al. 1980, 299).

These research findings illustrating the confounding effects of age on the comparison of transitions to widowhood and divorce evidently support the need for "the simultaneous study of a group of widows and divorcees in the same community who are matched on age," in order to avoid problems of competing explanations because of differences in sample size, age, study locations, and methodology (Kitson et al. 1980, 299). The few studies comparing widowhood and divorce in later life have used "truncated samples," not ones that include both younger and older persons (Roach and Kitson 1989), and this complicates the interpretation of research findings.

The Ontario widowhood study included a small sample of separated and divorced individuals who were interviewed using the same instrument (with appropriate modifications) and research design as for the widowhood study. The panel study from which both the widowed and the separated/divorced samples were drawn included 26 separated or divorced individuals, 19 of whom participated in the study.

The sample of separated/divorced elderly included 11 men and 8 women, separated or divorced an average of 9 years, and with an average age of 68 years. In Hyman's terms, they represent a somewhat "impure" sample for comparison with the widowed, as some had in fact experienced widowhood. Two had been widowed and then separated in their second marriage; one had been widowed in the first marriage and divorced in the second. In this sample, 53 percent were separated, and the average duration of the marriage to the first spouse was 24 years. For 68 percent, the former spouse was still alive, and was seen an average of several times a year. What the widowed and the separated/divorced share is having undergone a marital transition. Where they differ is in the experience of bereavement in their most recent marriage. Thus a comparison of the two "will help to specify whether the way of becoming single has effect over and above just being single and older" (Hennon 1983, 150).

Just as Kitson et al. (1980) have shown for the United States, so too a Statistics Canada survey has shown for Canada that the age distribution of widowed and divorced individuals differs, with more individuals being divorced at younger ages and widowed at older ages. In a national survey of 3,130 Canadians over the age of 65,[1] there were 1,187 widowed persons and 124 separated/divorced. Forty-two percent of the separated/divorced were between the ages of 65 and 69, compared to 21 percent of the widowed; 15 percent of the separated/divorced were over age 80, compared to 29 percent of the widowed. In the Ontario study, the widowed were an average age of 75, and the divorced an average age of 68 years. Because of the differing age distributions of the widowed and the divorced, one competing explanation for any observed differences in social support is the differences in the ages of the two groups. The older respondents, regardless of marital status, may respond differently to the items than do the younger respon-

TABLE 5.1

DEMOGRAPHIC PATTERNS: MARITAL STATUS COMPARISONS

Measure	Widowed $n = 152$		Separated/Divorced $n = 19$		Never Married $n = 62$	
	X̄	s.d.	X̄	s.d.	X̄	s.d.
Socio-economic Status	40.7	15.8	41.7	17.1	40.8	15.9
Household Income***	5.1	5.7	1.5	4.2	10.1	4.9
Education***	3.5	1.7	3.3	1.9	5.1	2.1
Living Siblings*	2.4	1.9	2.0	1.8	1.6	1.8
Living Relatives**	1.8	1.8	0.5	0.8	5.3	1.7
Friends***	1.8	1.6	1.7	1.7	5.0	2.0

   *   Widowed and never married are different at $p \leq .05$ level.
  ** Widowed, separated/divorced, and never married are different from each other at the $p \leq .05$ level.
 *** Never married are different from the widowed and separated/divorced at $p \leq .05$ level.

SOURCE: Martin Matthews.

dents. Because the two samples differed on age, this was statistically controlled in the analyses.

Table 5.1 compares the marital status groups on a range of demographic variables. There was only one statistically significant difference between the separated/divorced and the widowed. That was in the number of living relatives, with the widowed naming approximately three times as many relatives as did the separated/divorced. The implications of this finding are discussed further in the analysis of social support.

The lack of differences on several of these dimensions is in fact surprising. There was, for example, no distinction on the basis of socio-economic status as measured by the Blishen index of occupations, based on 1981 Canadian census data (Blishen et al. 1987). This index is based on characteristics of the entire employed labour force in 1981, using indicators of prevailing education and income levels. It provides a "unidimensional, contextual indicator which locates individuals in the Canadian occupational hierarchy at a given point in time" (1987, 473). The lower the score, the lower the socio-economic status. Even more surprising was the lack of significant distinction between the widowed and the separated/divorced on the income measures. Uhlenberg and Myers (1981) have noted that as a result of the division of property in a divorce settlement, both persons in the divorce can experience a substantial decline in their economic well-being. Particularly among the women in this sample, the separated/divorced actually had higher incomes than did the widowed, but this difference was not statistically significant. This finding is in contrast with research findings

TABLE 5.2

PERCEIVED SOCIAL SUPPORT: MARITAL STATUS COMPARISONS
(INTERPERSONAL SUPPORT EVALUATION LIST)

Measure	Widowed $n = 152$		Separated/Divorced $n = 19$		Never Married $n = 62$	
	$\overline{X}$	s.d.	$\overline{X}$	s.d.	$\overline{X}$	s.d.
Appraisal Support	11.8	1.9	12.3	1.9	11.5	1.9
Tangible Support	8.8	1.3	8.8	1.5	8.6	1.2
Belonging Support	11.5	1.8	12.3	2.4	11.4	1.6
Esteem Support*	16.2	1.5	16.5	1.3	15.4	2.3
Total ISEL	42.8	4.7	43.8	5.0	41.4	4.2

* Widowed and never married are different at $p \leq .05$ level.

SOURCE: Martin Matthews.

that divorce has stronger socio-economic consequences for women than does widowhood (Uhlenberg et al. 1990).

In examining the issue of the patterns of social support across marital status groups, the three measures of social support described in Chapter 4 are again utilized: perceived support, patterns of support, and sources of support. There were no statistically significant differences between the separated/divorced and the widowed elderly on the individual subscale measures of perceived social support, where a low score denotes high levels of perceived support. Both groups indicated high levels of perceived support overall, and relatively high levels of perceived tangible, belonging, and appraisal support. Whatever their varying objective circumstances, both the divorced and the widowed elderly felt that support was available to them, across most dimensions.

TABLE 5.3

PATTERNS OF SOCIAL SUPPORT: MARITAL STATUS COMPARISONS

Measure	Widowed $n = 152$		Separated/Divorced $n = 19$		Never Married $n = 62$	
	$\overline{X}$	s.d.	$\overline{X}$	s.d.	$\overline{X}$	s.d.
Numbers of Supporters						
Functional Children	1.8	1.4	1.7	1.3	—	—
Functional Siblings	0.7	1.1	0.5	0.7	0.9	1.2
Functional Relatives *	0.9	1.3	0.2	0.4	0.9	1.0
Functional Friends	1.3	1.3	0.6	0.8	1.0	1.1
Total Functional Contacts ****	4.7	2.6	3.0	1.9	2.9	1.7
Face-to-Face Contacts						
Children	0.9	1.2	1.0	1.3	—	—
Siblings	0.8	1.4	0.5	0.7	0.6	1.3
Other Relatives	0.9	1.5	0.2	0.5	0.6	0.9
Friends	0.7	1.1	1.0	1.6	1.1	1.1
Total ***	3.4	2.9	2.7	2.1	2.3	1.8
Telephone Contacts						
Children	1.5	1.7	1.8	1.4	—	—
Siblings	1.1	1.4	1.1	1.6	1.0	1.2
Other Relatives **	0.8	1.2	0.2	0.4	1.0	1.0
Friends	1.0	1.3	0.5	0.8	1.0	1.3
Total ***	4.4	3.1	3.5	2.3	2.9	2.2

   * Widowed and separated/divorced are different at $p \leq .05$ level.
  ** Separated/divorced and never married are different at $p \leq .05$ level.
 *** Widowed and never married are different at $p \leq .05$ level.
**** Widowed are different from the separated/divorced and never married at $p \leq .05$ level.

SOURCE: Martin Matthews.

Table 5.3 illustrates the findings with respect to patterns of social support in widowhood. There were significant differences between the separated/divorced and the widowed elderly in the actual numbers of individuals available to them as functional [2] members of their support networks. The widowed had significantly more functional relatives, friends, and total functional contacts than did the divorced.

For face-to-face contacts, the trend continues. The widowed averaged just over three individuals with whom they had regular direct contact. Among these, the widowed had more relatives with whom they had direct personal contact that did the separated/divorced. For telephone contacts, a similar pattern emerges, again showing that the widowed had slightly more contact with support network members. Widows and widowers had somewhat more telephone contact with extended family than did the separated/divorced elderly.

These data suggest that on at least one measure of support, patterns of support, the separated/divorced exhibited very different patterns from the widowed. Overall, the widowed had significantly more functional supporters in their networks. These differences are particularly evident in terms of extended-family contact. It is clear that research findings from one formerly married group in later life — the widowed — cannot be generalized to another—the separated/divorced. Their circumstances in later life, and the family dynamics characterizing their respective situations, differ markedly.

It is also clear that some of the separated/divorced found their own circumstance more difficult than they imagined widowhood to be. A third of the sample felt that divorce was more difficult and that widowhood would represent more of a resolution to the end of a marriage than did their present circumstance.

> I would feel much differently as a widow. There is such difficulty dealing with rejection. As a widow I would handle 'the separation' differently. It would be easier if he were dead in reference to family get-togethers. When my husband showed up with his girlfriend at my son's, I found it very traumatic. I wouldn't go to any function I knew he was going to attend. I am still friends with his brothers and sisters so it makes it very hard, socially. [Woman aged 64, separated 10 years]

While 16 percent felt there was no difference in the two transitions, 4 percent felt that it was harder to be widowed. Overall, the review of the literature and the examination of primary data from the Ontario survey suggest that, on many of the indicators of social support and well-being, the separated/divorced fared somewhat worse than did the widowed. The normative nature of widowhood appears to ease the transition for many; and likely because of the presumed lack of acrimony in family relations, the widowed enjoy the support of a broader and more involved network of family and friends.

A final point of comparison between the widowed and the separated/divorced is worthy of comment. An Australian study of 298 widowed women noted "the greater social acceptability of widowhood...shown by several women who volunteered as 'widows' for our study but who, on further inquiry, disclosed that they were either divorced or deserted" (Rosenman et al. 1981, 31). A similar pattern was observed in the Ontario research. Indeed, the impetus for the study of the separated/divorced came when two individuals who had previously described themselves as widowed were approached for the widowhood study and then disclosed that they were in fact separated. Rosenman et al. speculate that the elderly divorced or separated are so stigmatized that they have even more limited social supports than the widowed. The Ontario findings support such a view.

Overall, the research findings of the Ontario widowhood study indicate that while widowhood and divorce are "similar loss situations" (Lund 1989a), patterns of emotional response to the loss and patterns of contact with members of the social support network may be quite different between the two. However, because of the methodological problems characterizing much of the research comparing these marital status groups, caution must be exercised in the interpretation of research findings. When comparing the elderly widowed and divorced, future studies will need to be more sensitive to issues of the voluntary versus involuntary nature of the loss; the length of time between the termination of the marriage and the research interview; the rather different age distributions of the two marital status groups; and patterns of attrition in both populations due to death and remarriage (Kitson et al. 1989).

WIDOWHOOD VERSUS SINGLEHOOD

A comparison between the widowed and the never married or ever single is difficult because "never-marrieds constitute a particularly under-researched area" and thus "any conclusions [about them] would be hazardous at this time" (Chappell et al. 1986, 79). However, a brief comparison is important because of what it may convey about those aspects of widowhood in later life that represent relative desolation or deprivation rather than correlates of being "unattached" *per se*. Few comparisons between the widowed and the never married exist in the literature, largely because widowhood is frequently conceptualized as a life course transition and, by comparison, "there are no rites of passage for never-married women" (Allen 1989, 13). In addition, while the widowed and the separated/divorced may feel "mutually hostile" (Lopata 1979, 382) when comparisons are drawn between them, the widowed have been found to be genuinely puzzled by comparisons between their lives and those of the never married (Allen 1989). In an in-depth qualitative study of the lives of 15 widowed and

15 never-married women from the 1910 cohort, Allen found that the two marital status groups differed in their retrospective assessments of their lives.

> Most of the widows perceived that they had experienced all that life offered. More of the never-married expressed regrets about their lives or perceived that their lives were uneventful and dull. The widows had lived what they considered to be the acceptable lifestyle for women. [Allen 1989, 126]

Although modest in scope, several Canadian studies have compared the widowed and the never married. One study contrasted the patterns of social involvement of widows with that of never-married older women. The mean age of the sample was 71 years, and the widowed had experienced an average of ten years since the death of their spouse (Norris 1980). The widows were more socially engaged than were the never married primarily because of their involvement in kinship roles. On the other hand, the never married were more adjusted and happier in old age. Differences between the two groups reflect involvement in the role of wife or worker that has been maintained beyond the loss of the role.

Comparisons of data on social support were similarly made between the findings of the Ontario widowhood study and the study of 62 never-married older men and women in rural and urban Ontario. The findings on the never-married population showed a bipolar pattern of characteristics among this group: most were far better off than the widowed on various attributes, while others were far worse off. Tables 5.1, 5.2, and 5.3 compare the widowed and the never married on demographic and social support measures. On demographic measures of income and education, and on the overall measure of perceived social support and patterns of support, never-married women in particular are typically better off than are widowed or separated/divorced women. Quite the reverse is true for never-married men, who consistently report lower levels of income, education, and support than do either widowers or separated/divorced men.

However, two very different profiles of never-married women emerge from this comparison. One population, the more typical of the two, consists of women who are very well educated, have higher-than-average incomes, good health, very high levels of morale and well-being, and who psychologically and socially appear to be as well off as the widowed, if not better off. The other population of single women, more closely approximating the profile of single men, is characterized by poorer health, below-average levels of education, very low levels of income, and smaller and more tenuous support networks. While of course heterogeniety characterizes any population whose only common attribute is marital status, the extreme diversity of the never-married population is particularly striking, and is not true of the widowed.

Overall, there were as many similarities as differences between the widowed and the never married on specific aspects of their patterns of support and the perception of support. On the measure of the ISEL (where a low score denotes high levels of perceived support), the widowed reported a significantly lower level of esteem support than did the never married. This measure reflects the availability of others to promote a sense of value and self-worth. On the measure of patterns of support (Table 5.3), the widowed had significantly more total functional contacts, total face-to-face contacts, and total telephone contacts than did the never married. The never marrieds' lack of children perhaps overemphasizes their comparative disadvantage when only the *total* numbers of functional contacts are considered. In comparisons of only those family and friend relationships that are in fact available to members of all three marital status groups, the never married demonstrate patterns of social support very similar to those of the widowed. On measures of sources of support, the never married showed more reliance than did the widowed on siblings as helpers in times of illness or when tangible support was needed, although they had fewer living siblings and fewer functional contacts overall than did the widowed. Otherwise, these two marital status groups were more like one another than like the separated/divorced.

MULTIPLE STATUS PASSAGES

In the process of experiencing transitional life events, individuals undergo status passages. While frequently these passages are sequential, they sometimes occur simultaneously, overlapping wholly or in part. These "multiple status passages" (Glaser and Strauss 1971) may support each other (as when a new parent leaves the labour force for a time to adapt to the parent role) or they may be competing. Among the status passages that widowed individuals may experience are retirement and involvement in caregiving roles.

Work and Retirement

Most older women in Canada belong to a generation in which only a small proportion ever held jobs outside their homes. Even for cohorts now entering old age, retirement from the paid labour force is not a typical life course transition for most women. In addition, when women do retire from employment outside the home, a sizeable proportion do so before age 65, and thus before widowhood. For example, 34 percent of women aged 55 to 64 were in the paid labour force in 1983 (Statistics Canada 1985a, 48). By contrast, in 1975, 46 percent of women aged 45 to 54 were in the paid labour force. These figures suggest that about a quarter of middle-aged women in the labour force in 1975 actually retired before reaching age 64 — very likely because of the retirement of their spouse. It is not until we consider the group of women now aged 45 to 54, 58 percent of whom were in the paid labour force in 1983, that we can expect retirement to be a transition which most Canadian women will personally experience.

In the recent past, women's rate of participation in the paid labour force has shown dramatic change, increasing from 38 to 53 percent between 1970 and 1983 (Statistics Canada 1985a, 41). The number of female workers increased by more than 70 percent to 4.8 million (Health and Welfare Canada 1983, 34). Much of women's employment in Canada remains part time. In 1983, almost 1.2 million women, representing just over one-quarter of the female labour force, worked part time. Income is another factor that has profound implications for women's pensions and hence their economic status in retirement and widowhood. The 1982 average earnings of women who were employed full time were $16,100, representing just 64 percent of the earnings of full-time male employees. However, there has been progress in this area, albeit slow: a decade earlier, women's average annual earnings were just under 60 percent of those of men (Statistics Canada 1985a, 46).

While there has been much discussion in Canada (Government of Canada 1979; Parliamentary Task Force on Pension Reform 1983) of ways to improve the financial circumstances of older women in retirement, particularly those who are unattached, gains are not likely to be made in the near future. Discussions of pensions for homemakers have been fraught with controversy. In the private sector in 1979 only 30 percent of females (compared with 49 percent of males) were members of employer-sponsored pension plans (Health and Welfare Canada 1982, 6), and few such plans have survivor benefits. Moreover, in excess of two million women work in the private sector, earning less than the average wage, and have no private pension protection at all. A factor that does not bode well for the future of women's financial status in retirement is that only one-third of females in the private sector, in the 25 to 44 and 45 to 64 age groups, were members of pension plans in 1979. A recognition of these financial issues is important when considering the multiple status passages of widowhood and retirement, for economic changes accompanying retirement are an important aspect of this life course transition.

Researchers have only recently begun to examine the extent to which retirement is differentially experienced by women and by men, and there is little Canadian material on this topic. A Manitoba study of 140 retirees, including 62 men and 78 women, found that widowhood was one of the factors associated with dissatisfaction in retirement (Browning and Bond 1987). It also found that retired women were more likely to be widowed and in poorer financial condition than were men.

Research on this topic has generally been couched in terms of an ongoing debate about whether retirement is more difficult for women or for men. Connidis has, however, made the valid point that "a more fruitful approach to the entire question rests in considering male-female differences in the process of adjustment to retirement instead of attempting to determine who is better at it" (1982, 19). An Ontario study examined the patterns of adaptation of 300 persons between the ages of 60 and 72, retired for more than one year but not more than five years. In this study 124 of the respondents were women. The men and women differed in their reasons for retirement, with men more likely to retire for reasons of company policy (37 percent versus 22 percent), or being tired of work. Men and women were equally likely to retire for health reasons, with about a quarter of each group doing so. Perhaps as a forewarning of impending widowhood, women were much more likely than men to retire for reasons of the declining health of their spouse or other family member (7 percent of women versus 1 percent of men). Eight percent of the women, but none of the men, retired because of the retirement of their spouse. While the majority defined retirement as a generally positive experience, there were differences between men and women in this regard. Nearly two-thirds (62 percent) of the men but only 45 percent of the women reported that their feelings at the time of retirement were essentially positive (Martin Matthews and Brown 1987; Martin Matthews and Tindale 1987).

Canadian research by Roadburg (1985) also found that men and women specifically identified several facets of their work lives which they missed in retirement. Nearly half the men (44 percent) and two-thirds of the women (67 percent) missed the social contact that work provided, while over half the men (52 percent) and just over one-fifth of the women (21 percent) missed having something to do. Roadburg (1985) explained these gender differences by noting that, since a smaller proportion of men live alone, they would be less likely to be lonely and miss the social contact of work. In addition, because the majority of these women who retired from paid employment would still be at least partially involved in housework, they would be less likely to miss having something to do.

Very little has been written on the retirement experiences of widowed women or the widowhood experiences of retired women. While there is some reference in the literature to the "double whammy" of widowhood and retirement occurring either close together or simultaneously, it is clear that this does not happen for most women. The usual pattern in Canada is for retirement before age 65, with widowhood occurring typically in the next five to ten years. One study of widowed and married retired women found that formal social participation, either as a voluntary association participant or as a volunteer worker, was related to satisfaction in retirement for women (Dorfman and Moffet 1987). The proportion of close friends retained from the pre-retirement period and frequency of contact with close friends and neighbours were positively related to life satisfaction during retirement for widowed women, but not for married women. In fact, the proportion of close friends retained from the pre-retirement years was the strongest predictor of life satisfaction among the widows. This suggests that not only frequency of contact with friends but also maintenance of friendships over time is important to retired widows (Dorfman and Moffet 1987).

Research findings on the relationship between adaptation to widowhood and participation in the paid labour force are inconclusive. DiGiulio (1989, 95) has described paid work as "the widow's solace and salvation," and U.S. national survey data have indicated that, for widowed women, employment roles are a direct source of positive affect (Arens 1982). However, other research found that the longer a woman had worked outside the home, the psychologically worse, rather than better, she felt at widowhood (McGloshen and O'Bryant 1988). Another study of the mid-life widowed noted three rather different patterns in relation to employment and widowhood. While some widowed persons found their jobs to be the one place providing them with a sense of support, security, and continuity in their lives, others found that their inability to function effectively in their jobs during their grieving exacerbated feelings of depression. Yet another group overinvested themselves in their jobs in order to avoid dealing with their grief and also to help find some meaning in their lives (Demi 1989, 237).

Caregiving Roles

The caregiving role is one with which most widowed people are well familiar. For most people in our society, not just the widowed, the role of caregiver is by no means a short-term responsibility. It is estimated that the average woman spends 17 years of her life caring for a dependent child and 18 years helping a dependent parent (Select Committee on Aging 1987, 66). Not included in this calculation is the amount of time spent caring for an ailing spouse. Given women's increased life expectancy, it is now entirely possible for an elderly woman to be actively involved as a caregiver to her very old and frail mother at the same time as she is caring for an ailing spouse or is herself already widowed. In other cases, the transition to widowhood is exacerbated by the continuing dependency of disabled family members for whom the widowed are responsible. Numerous cases of this were identified in the Ontario widowhood study, typically involving a child but occasionally a sibling.

> What the hell can I do? My son has been crippled since birth, I'm not the best one for him now, but I'm the one who's got the responsibility of him. I don't really have any choice in the matter. [Man aged 72, widowed 6 years]

> Since my husband died, I've looked after my invalid mother and an invalid mother-in-law. That made me more of a loner than anything. Because of it, I'm more independent and I count on myself more than others. [Woman aged 76, widowed one year]

However, the role of caring for an ailing spouse may in fact ease an individual — usually a woman — into the transition to widowhood. Rosenthal and Dawson, who have analysed this phenomenon in relation to the wives of the institutionalized, refer to the situation of "quasi-widowhood," where the woman must accept "the loss of the person who was her full-time spouse, and [learn]...to live as a woman alone whose husband still lives" (forthcoming, 21).

Women in the Ontario widowhood study spoke of how the performance of the caregiving role facilitated their adjustment to the eventual loss of their spouse.

> Widowhood didn't make too much difference to me personally. My husband hadn't been very well for a number of years. [Woman aged 77, widowed 5 years]
>
> My husband was sick for a couple of years so I got used to being independent. [Woman aged 76, widowed 2 years]
>
> He wasn't able to do any jobs as far as keeping up the house. I did it all so there was no change that way. [Woman aged 67, widowed one year]

These observations provide valuable insight into the experience of widowhood in later life. Not only do they illustrate the importance of the caregiving role as part of the process of anticipatory socialization for widowhood, but they also underscore the importance of the relative placement of transitional life events within a social context. Pearlin observed that the sheer number and magnitude of life course changes such as widowhood are less important to emotional states than is the manner in which these changes are consonant or conflict with other features of one's life. "It is not the passages that matter; it is, rather, the nature of the contexts from which we have departed and those that we discover at our destinations" (Pearlin 1980, 351). The experience of widowhood will, therefore, be quite different if it occurs within the context of a lengthy or intensive caregiving role. Some individuals may feel quite bereft, now being without either a spouse or a nursing role (Willis et al. 1987), while others may experience profound relief. Indeed, it has been argued that what appears to be a stressful life event, such as widowhood, may in fact be far from stressful. After a bad marriage or an extensive period of caregiving, for example, the loss of the spouse "spells the end of the chronic stress involved" (Wortman and Silver 1990, 258).

Competing role demands associated with retirement and caregiving may have both short- and long-term implications for the transition to later-life widowhood. The experience of retirement with its attendant loss of the social world of work may exacerbate the loneliness of widowhood for some. This may be particularly true of those who sought work as a refuge from the travails of bereavement. In other cases, however, successful adaptation to the loss of the work role may serve as a model of individual coping mechanisms in the face of transition.

Responsibilities associated with caregiving, especially for an aged parent or dependent adult child, may prove particularly burdensome for those also experiencing the transition to widowhood. On the other hand, the experience of caregiving for an ill spouse may serve for some as anticipatory socialization to the role of widowed person.

CONCLUSION

Most studies of the widowed do not include control groups of those who have not experienced the loss of the spouse, or of those who have experienced other kinds of losses. As a result, conclusions that any observed patterns are in fact due to widowhood may be questionable. The comparison of data from three Ontario studies of the widowed, the separated/divorced, and the never married permit the identification of those features of social support and well-being that truly are unique to the widowed.

In comparison with the divorced, the widowed have many more functional supporters in their networks, particularly in terms of extended-family contact. The normative nature of widowhood appears to ease the transition, with mental health outcomes being rather better for the widowed than for the divorced.

Overall, there were as many similarities as differences between the widowed and the never married on specific aspects of their patterns of support and the perception of support. The widowed reported significantly lower levels of esteem support than did the never married. This measure reflects the availability of others to promote a sense of value and self-worth. On measures of sources of support, the never married indicated more reliance than did the widowed on siblings as helpers, although they had fewer living siblings and fewer functional contacts overall than did the widowed. Otherwise, these two marital status groups were somewhat more similar to one another than to the separated/divorced.

Competing role demands associated with the performance of other roles or the experience of simultaneous transitions may have an impact on the experience of widowhood in later life. While the experience of retirement from the paid labour force is rarely coincident with widowhood, the loss of ongoing contact with work associates may exacerbate the loneliness of widowhood for some individuals. The burdens of caregiving for dependent adult children or disabled parents may also complicate the transition to widowhood. For some widowed persons, however, a lengthy period of caregiving for an ailing spouse may provide opportunities for anticipatory socialization to the role of widowed person.

In the next chapter, several demographic trends that will likely have an impact on the experience of widowhood in the future are discussed. Policy implications of current characteristics of widowhood are addressed, as are outstanding research issues in the study of widowhood.

NOTES

1. The Canadian General Social Survey is a national survey conducted by Statistics Canada in 1985, and includes a sample of 3,130 elderly individuals: 1,593 were married; 1,187 were widowed; 226 were never married; and 124 were separated/divorced.
2. The definition of "functional" supports is provided in Chapter 4.

CHAPTER 6

RESEARCH DIRECTIONS AND POLICY ISSUES

Preceding chapters have documented the heterogeneity that characterizes the population who spend their later years as widowed people. In addition, the examination of Canadian research suggests that being younger, experiencing a brief final illness of the spouse, being male, and having a low income level exacerbate the transition to widowhood and the status of being a widowed person. It is also apparent that tremendous flux characterizes the pattern of social supports in the transition to widowhood, particularly in terms of friendship relations. In contrast with other research findings on widows (Lopata 1978; 1979), however, research findings in Canada show that the role of the extended family in the support networks of the widowed is quite striking. And finally, the importance of the personal resources of the widowed in shaping the reliance upon and response to social supports is supported by Canadian researchers.

FUTURE RESEARCH: SUBSTANTIVE ISSUES

While there is a growing body of Canadian research on the widowed, in contrast with the situation a decade ago (Martin Matthews 1980b), this area of research is still very much in its infancy. Many outstanding research questions remain. Specific subgroups of the widowed — identified by U.S. researchers as having somewhat distinct experiences of widowhood as a life event (those widowed off time and widowed members of minority ethnic groups) — have not been systematically studied in Canada. No Canadian research has specifically examined how the experience of widowhood may differ for members of Canada's two charter groups, the British and the French. Future Canadian research would also do well to attempt comparative analyses of men's and women's experiences of the transition to widowhood. While the numbers of widowed older men are small, there is evidence that the issues facing them are distinctly different from those facing women. And although some of these differences may be cohort related, it is important for policy planning and programme intervention to understand the particular patterns of social support utilized by elderly widowed men, as compared with women.

The context in which widowhood occurs, both environmental and personal, is also an important consideration. Many features of Canadian society that both contribute to our uniqueness as a nation and add potential complexity to the experience of widowhood have not been investigated in relation to widowhood in later life. These include bilingualism, multiculturalism, regional diversity, and the concentrations of the aged in rural areas. Although one might speculate on the implications of these national characteristics for the experience of widowhood, rigorous research is needed to elucidate specific relationships.

There are other features of Canadian society and of the place of the elderly widowed in that society, however, that are in flux. In the future development of a research agenda on later-life widowhood particular attention will need to be paid to these features, which include issues of the changing social roles of women, labour force participation and unemployment rates among older women, patterns of migration, and location in a rural versus an urban environment. These are discussed below.

As Lopata (1987b, 275) notes, today's elderly widowed women were socialized at a point in history "when women were supposed to limit themselves to the private, home sphere, and not to venture outside of it except to meet its needs. They were not expected to demand attention from the public sphere and its bureaucracies." In this sense, Lopata observes, newer generations of widowed women will not be facing many of the problems and restrictions typical of today's older widow (1987b).

Issues of labour force participation and rates of unemployment have a direct bearing on the availability of economic supports in widowhood. In recent years, Canada has witnessed a significant rate of growth in female labour force participation, particularly among middle-aged women. While this appears to augur well for the economic supports of the widowed, Dulude concluded that "almost two-thirds of widows in their fifties who are in the labour force hold low-paying unskilled jobs" (1979, 10). Data from the 1981 census of Canada show that while the labour force participation rate for females over the age of 15 as a whole is 52 percent, the participation rate for the widowed and the divorced female is 31 percent (Statistics Canada 1984). In addition, while mature women workers have a substantially lower rate of unemployment than their younger counterparts (in 1981 it was 7 percent for widowed and divorced women), the bad news is that "older women suffer longer periods of unemployment than do younger women" (1979, 11). Dulude observed that while this phenomenon had received very little attention in Canada, it had been extensively studied in the United States where "it was found to be at least partially due to age discrimination." Indeed, it has been generally acknowledged that "to be old and female is the best combination to ensure being poor in Canada...and to be old and a widow is an even better one" (1979, 40). The main cause of the widows' poverty is the extreme financial vulnerability of most elderly married women, at least one-third of whom have no personal income at all. Dulude further noted: "More than half of all married women aged 55 to 64 have no income at all. When their husbands die, it appears that most of them will inherit nothing other than poverty." These factors have significant impli- cations for the perpetuation of patterns of economic support available to the widowed woman in Canada, and reflect her reliance on savings and other forms of family-generated assistance in order to ensure her livelihood.

Another phenomenon with direct relevance to the social supports of the widowed is the high rate of migration characteristic of Canadian society. Nearly half (48 percent) of the Canadian population changed residence between 1976 and 1981; a fifth of Canadians (20 percent) moved from a different municipality, and 15 percent from a different province (Statistics Canada 1983). Although national data indicating the availability of children in geographical proximity to their elderly or widowed kin are not readily available, there is reason to believe that these high rates of mobility can and do have an impact on the availability of kin as resources in the social support networks of the widowed.

Another factor complicating the issue of mobility is the recognition that rates of out-migration are high among the young residents of rural areas, and that in these areas the elderly widowed in particular are overrepresented. For example, while widows constitute 12 percent of women living in urban areas, they constitute fully 18 percent of women residing in rural areas. Among widowed rural women, fully 93 percent reside in non-farm areas, typically small towns and villages. The demography of rural Canada suggests that this pattern will continue and likely even intensify in the future. For example, a Health and Welfare Canada report (1983, 26) notes: "Only 9.4 percent of the total population of large urban centres was age 65 and over in 1981...Small towns, on the other hand, had an unusually large proportion of elderly persons in their populations. In towns with 1,000 to 2,499 people, 13.5 percent of the population was aged 65 or more...."

Indeed, census data show that small towns have a larger-than-average proportion of persons aged 80 and over relative to their total population, 3 percent compared to the national average of 2 percent (Health and Welfare Canada 1983). In Chapter 1, Table 1.3 illustrates the proportions of widowed women in this age group. It is apparent that many rural areas of Canada have, and will continue to have, high concentrations of elderly widows in their populations. These environments are frequently characterized by few or no formalized support services for the aged and a reduced availability of younger family members as potential supports.

Also relevant to this discussion of circumstances associated with the availability of and access to supports are several demographic characteristics of Canada's current aged population. As Marshall has noted, "the cohort now in old age has very few children compared to earlier cohorts and also compared to most later cohorts. The cohort now in their forties has more children than the preceding and following cohorts" (Marshall 1981, 17-18). Since Marshall wrote almost a decade ago, his statement is true of those now in their fifties. As we have seen, Canada's aged women represent a substantial proportion of the widowed. Their extremely low birth rate therefore makes this cohort of widows fundamentally different from preceding and succeeding cohorts of widows in terms of their access to intergenerational family contacts as potential supports. The next generation of widowed persons, the parents of the "baby boom," will therefore have available to them more children but fewer of the other types of family supports described in these chapters. The succeeding generation of widowed will be the "baby boomers" themselves, who appear destined to have birth rates as low as, if not lower than, those of their grandparents. One future trend we might anticipate is the increased primacy of "fictive kin." Already we see that the widowed elderly are far more likely than the non-widowed to include non-family members in their descriptions of people whom they think of as "family." The nature of these friendship bonds in the lives of the aged have not been extensively studied (certainly not to the extent that family relations have been studied), but their potential importance is beyond question.

The future will also undoubtedly be characterized by many more individuals whose marriage(s) is/are terminated by separation and divorce rather than, or in addition to, the death of the spouse. There is preliminary evidence that separation, divorce, and remarriage are associated with different family dynamics from those associated with widowhood. We can only speculate on the experience of widowhood for individuals who have undergone divorce from a previous marriage. The question is whether anticipatory socialization through previous experience of the termination of a marriage significantly alters the patterns of response to widowhood.

Some researchers suggest that the prevalence of widowhood will in fact decrease fairly significantly because of a dramatic increase in divorce and because approximately one-third of divorced women never remarry (Hagestad 1988). Analyses of U.S. population trends suggest that "about half as many women in the more recent cohort [born 1955–59] will be widows at [age 65-69], but four times as many will be divorced (compared with the 1905-09 cohort when *they* were 65-69)" (Uhlenberg et al. 1990, S7). Projections are that, with a continuance of currently low rates of marriage and remarriage, about half of all women entering old age in 2025 will not be in any marriage. Indeed, the proportions of older women living outside marriage could be substantially higher if U.S. divorce rates after age 40 continue to increase while remarriage rates continue to decline (Uhlenberg et al. 1990). It is entirely possible, therefore, that among cohorts of currently married women, widowhood could in fact become a quite non-normative status in later life.

In addition, the definition of widowhood, in both legal and social terms, will need to change to reflect the increasing prevalence of common-law marriages. Since 1981, the number of reported common-law unions increased in Canada by 38 percent. In 1986, 8 percent of all couples (about 487,000) reported their union was not based on a legal marriage, up from 6 percent or about 352,000 couples in 1981 (Devereaux 1988, 25).

In sum, a range of socio-economic and cohort-related factors influence the experience of widowhood in Canadian society. Not the least of these for the group of aged widows who have been the focus of this analysis is the fact that the very nature of widowhood has changed in terms of its location and duration in the life course of women. "Widowhood is now a typical family life course stage for women, located at the end of the life course. In an earlier era — as recently as for the cohorts born in the last quarter of the nineteenth century — many more women could expect to die in childbirth, or to either predecease their husbands or to enter widowhood at a much younger age" (Marshall 1981, 21).

FUTURE RESEARCH: METHODOLOGICAL ISSUES

Highest priority must be given to the examination of widowhood as a process of transition, rather than as merely a status held by most older women. For example, in examining the nature of social support in widowhood, Canadian studies primarily focus on the supportive relationships of those who currently hold the status of widowed person. There has been relatively little research on the way in which social relationships and support networks influence and are themselves changed by the *process* of becoming widowed. Studies have also typically examined the what and the how of the reconstructed social world in widowhood, but not the actual process of reconstruction. Research that more fully addresses the social meaning of widowhood for men and women is certainly needed. Widowhood has also frequently been studied in isolation from other aspects of the life course of individuals, even though no single stage of a person's life can be understood apart from its antecedents and consequences. The past decade has seen a growth in widowhood research in Canada. A realistic and worthwhile goal for the future is the completion of more comprehensive and process-oriented research on widowhood in later life. For this, of course, longitudinal research is required. The Canadian, and many of the U.S. and international, research findings reported in this monograph have been derived for the most part from small, cross-sectional studies in a variety of local settings.

Largely because of the cross-sectional nature of much of the research, another characteristic of the study of widowhood that limits what we can know through utilizing a life course perspective is the persistent habit of studying role transitions *after* the transitional event. This approach very much influences our knowledge about the nature of a transitional life event such as widowhood. Role transitions that are embedded in the life course can be predicted far in advance of the actual occurrence of the transitions themselves. Their very predictability, in turn, means that adjustment to these changes can begin to take place prior to the onset of the changes themselves.

Prospective and longitudinal studies during married couples' later years are therefore required so as to better understand the relationships between illness, caregiving, dying, and the transition to widowhood (O'Bryant 1990). Researchers have noted in particular: the need for more information about how the deaths of other family members and friends affect the preparedness of older married couples (*ibid.*); the need for the manipulation of crucial variables involving family functioning and dynamics in order to test cause and effect relationships (Bohm and Rodin 1985); and the need for longitudinal studies with shorter intervals between measurement periods, over a longer time, and beginning before the spouse's death (Lund 1986a). A pioneering attempt at this kind of prospective research on widowhood is currently underway in the United States (Wortman and Silver 1990). Baseline data are collected on respondents at risk for bereavement (where the spouse is over the age of 65), and these data are used to assess, prior to loss, potential risk factors, confounding variables, and coping resources such as social support.

Issues of sample selection are also of concern in the study of widowhood. Samples of widowed respondents are typically identified through clinical case-loads, death records, localized sample surveys of the widowed, localized sample surveys of the aged, and secondary analyses of nationwide sample surveys (Hyman 1983). Each of these sampling procedures has its own inherent methodological strengths and weaknesses.

In a review of 52 articles reporting the results of research on widowhood, Gentry and Shulman (1985) found that 21 percent were based on archival or secondary analyses of data; 12 percent used samples identified through death records; and 27 percent did not report their sample selection procedures. Most alarming in their view was the fact that "40 percent of all the studies of widowhood in this survey used convenience samples such as widow-to-widow groups or referrals from acquaintances" (Gentry and Shulman (1985, 642). Other researchers have similarly decried the heavy reliance on convenience samples and noted the difficulties in recruiting subjects for widowhood research (Kitson et al. 1989).

The general lack of rigour in widowhood research in terms of the failure to report sampling frame, sampling procedures, or both (Gentry and Shulman 1985), and the preponderance of studies using convenience samples, contribute to potential bias in research findings. Hyman (1983), for example, has contended that in studies where respondents are contacted because they hold a particular status, higher salience is given to that particular role identity than is the case among persons contacted through random sampling techniques. This heightened salience, Hyman suggests, provides a distorted view. While some researchers suggest that samples based on public death records produce the fewest biases, they also concede that these records do not permit the analysis of processes leading up to the death, "a period that needs further study" (Kitson et al. 1989, 22). In addition to being as unbiased as possible, samples used in widowhood research in the future will need to be large enough to permit multivariate analyses, and heterogeneous enough to permit cross-cultural comparisons "to help identify the universal and unique features of bereavement" (Lund 1989a).

As the following section on policy issues indicates, the issue of the uniqueness of the experience of widowhood in later life is also increasingly being questioned. Much of the research conducted on the widowed has not involved comparisons with individuals of other marital statuses. This lack of comparisons prevents a clear explanation of which characteristics are in fact unique to the widowed. Methodological weaknesses characterize much of the published literature on marital status comparisons. In addition to problems of small sample size and undifferentiated age range, another problem involves the collapsing of the marital status categories together. In some studies, the single, the separated/divorced, and the widowed are treated as one category of "unattached" persons, while in others the widowed are analyzed as a distinct group, and in yet others all the unattached statuses are separated out for analysis. There are real dangers in these analysis strategies. In terms of life histories and the potential availability of certain kinds of kin (children, grandchildren, in-laws, and so forth), the separated/divorced may be quite unlike the never married, who may in turn be rather different from the widowed. The collapsing of coding categories for marital status in this manner does not allow the scientific determination of what differences exist, and how potentially significant they may be.

Another methodological problem affecting surveys of the widowed involves response bias and patterns of non-response. Gentry and Shulman (1985) found that only 19 percent of studies gave information necessary to determine what percentage of the targeted widows and widowers actually participated. Kitson et al. (1989) similarly noted the lack of uniformity across studies of widowhood in reporting completion and refusal rates, and the particular problems of attrition in longitudinal research. Although prospective and longitudinal studies are called for by widowhood researchers, sample attrition is a stark reality with this type of data collection: a two-year study of 192 bereaved individuals studied at six measurement periods found that only 56 percent of the respondents completed the survey at all data-collection phases (Caserta et al. 1985). Although one potential source of response bias, repeated interaction with interviewers for widowhood research projects, has not been found to affect outcomes (ibid.), systematic differences have been noted between participants in a bereavement study and those who refused. Researchers suggest that those who refused to participate were probably functioning more poorly (Lehman et al. 1987). Patterns of non-response and response bias pose problems for the interpretation of findings and for the generalizability of results, particularly "the murky question of evaluating the loss of those so badly affected that they cannot talk about their bereavement and the inclusion of those so affected that they seize the opportunity to talk about it" (Hyman 1983, 8).

SOCIAL POLICY ISSUES

As noted by Connidis in *Family Ties and Aging* (1989b), another volume in this Series, the problems that individuals experience can be treated as "personal troubles" to be dealt with privately by those directly involved, or they can be generalized as "public issues" of concern to society as a whole (Mills 1959, 8). While many of the characteristics of widowhood in later life as described in this monograph are considered personal troubles, other characteristics, particularly those related to financial support, have come to be defined as public issues governed by public policy and legislation. Connidis cited widowhood as a "good example" of the application of public policy in the area of family issues. As she noted, while the "intensely personal process of bereavement...[is]...a private trouble to be surmounted by the widow..., some of the repercussions of widowhood, such as the poverty experienced by many widows, are more accurately considered public issues because they are, at least in part, socially created" (1989b, 92).

The acceptance of societal responsibility for the economic security of the widowed has been a comparatively recent event. The establishment of the Old Age Security program in Canada, the introduction of the Canada/Quebec Pension Plan, and the extension of the Guaranteed Income Supplement all represent public policy initiatives that recognize society's responsibilities to its aged citizens and attempt to secure a basic level of economic security for them. Until quite recently, however, this provision of support had a particularly cruel twist for the widowed. Published accounts exist of newly widowed women receiving notices from federal authorities expressing regret at the recent death of their spouse, and informing them that his Old Age Security benefits would cease immediately. Efforts were then made to redress this situation. It was felt that individuals in the "near elderly" years between the ages 55 and 64 were particularly hard hit financially by widowhood, as they did not qualify for any public pension benefits nor were they at a point in their lives when participation in the paid labour force was a viable or available option for them. In recognition of this fact, various federal and provincial initiatives were undertaken.

One such program is the federal Widowed Spouse's Allowance, designed to financially assist low-income widowed persons aged 60 to 64. This benefit is subject to an income test, based on individual income in the preceding calendar year, and is discontinued when the widowed person reaches age 65 and thereby becomes eligible for other public pensions, or when the widowed person remarries. The only other eligibility requirements are that the individual must have resided in Canada for at least ten years after reaching age 18 and must have fulfilled the citizenship or legal residence requirements (Income Security Programs 1987a, 1987b). This program has evolved over a ten-year period. It was implemented in 1975 under the Old Age Security Act as a Spouse's Allowance to provide assistance in the special case where both members of a couple were trying to live on one public pension benefit. In such cases, one spouse was over the age of 65 and receiving benefits; the younger spouse aged 60-64 thus also became eligible to receive benefits under this income-tested program. Three years later, legislation was effected to continue the Spouse's Allowance benefits for six months following the death of the pensioner spouse. This legislation recognized for the first time as a policy issue the near-elderly widowed person's financial insecurity. A year later in 1979, the period of eligibility was extended until the widowed spouse reached age 65, remarried, or died. In 1985, the benefits were extended to all low-income widowed persons aged 60 to 64, regardless of when their spouse had died. This change made the benefit available to a substantially larger group of widowed persons. Prior to that, it was only available to those whose spouse was receiving Old Age Security benefits at the time of his or her death. With the extension of the legislation, even those whose spouses had died many years previously now became eligible for the income-tested allowance. Application for the allowance must be made on an annual basis.

At the same time that these legislative initiatives were being undertaken at the federal level, a Widows' Pension Act was also passed in Alberta (Government of the Province of Alberta 1983). This income-tested allowance is available to Alberta widows and widowers aged 55 to 64 who meet the citizenship and residency requirements. It provides a monthly pension as well as premium-free Alberta Health Care Insurance, extended health benefits, a property education tax reduction or equivalent, and eligibility for home improvement and home heating grants.

In addition to these policy initiatives directed specifically towards the widowed, legal reforms in various Canadian provinces have also fundamentally changed family law, with wide-ranging implications for widowed men and women. While the legislation associated with such reform is a provincial responsibility, and hence will vary from one province to the next, an overview of legislative provisions in Canada's most populous province, Ontario, illustrates several implications of this reform for the widowed. The *Ontario Succession Law Reform Act* (R.S.O. 1980, c. 488) for example, governs the right of surviving spouses and other family members on the death of a family member. If a person dies without a will, the surviving spouse receives the first $75,000 of the estate plus half of any remainder if there is one child, or one-third of the remainder if there are two or more children. If there are no children, the surviving spouse receives the entire estate. If the deceased left a will, the surviving family members receive what the will says is to go to them. However, if this is inadequate, they can apply to a court for a greater share of the estate. This right is available to the spouse, parents, children, brothers, and sisters of the deceased if the deceased was supporting them or was under a legal obligation to support them (Schlesinger 1979, 190).

However, policy initiatives targeted towards the widowed are currently being affected by the introduction of the *Canadian Charter of Rights and Freedoms* (enacted as Schedule B to the *Canada Act, 1982* (U.K.) 1982, c. 11) which came into effect in April 1985. Under provisions related to equality, "every individual is equal before and under the law and has the right to the equal protection and equal benefit of the law without discrimination and, in particular, without discrimination based on race, national or ethnic origin, colour, religion, sex, age or mental or physical ability" (Government of Canada 1982, 15). The implementation of these provisions on equality rights means that "For the first time in Canadian history, the Constitution will make it clear that, for women, equality is not a right to be acquired, but a state that exists. It will ensure that women are entitled to full equality in law — and not just in the laws themselves but in the administration of law as well" (Government of Canada 1982, 16).

As a test of the equality provisions of the *Charter*, litigation challenging policies targeted towards the widowed has been initiated at the federal and provincial levels on the grounds of discrimination on the basis of marital status (Personal communication, Health and Welfare Canada; Personal communication, Office of the Attorney General, Government of Alberta). Individuals and groups such as Single and Divorced Speak Out have launched these challenges because, although they meet income and age criteria for the programs, they do not qualify because they never married or their spouse died after the termination of the marriage through divorce (Livingstone 1988). One divorced member of a group challenging the special programs for the widowed questions the assumptions underlying the programs: "'They say a widow has a hard time of it. The only difference is we have no body to bury. We still ...continue grieving for the rest of our lives.'" Says another single person, "'There seems to be an attitude ... that a widow or widower is a superior person to someone who is single or divorced. It really glorifies marriage'" (ibid.). These challenges raise the significant issue of the extent to which the widowed as a group are indeed any more disadvantaged overall than are individuals who are similarly "unattached" in later life for reasons of divorce or singlehood. At the time of writing, no legal judgements had been made in any of these cases.

In addition to litigation, other challenges face public policy initiatives directed towards the widowed. In a climate of national fiscal restraint and deficit cutting, concerns have arisen about potential changes to the Widowed Spousal Allowance, changes that "would substantially increase the spousal benefit, but make it payable in full for only three years and phase it out entirely over the next two" (Shifrin 1988, A15). While these recommended changes have not been implemented, they do point to the potential fragility of programs on which the widowed may have come to rely.

CONCLUSION

This examination of widowhood in later life has focused on issues of adaptation, social support, and variability in the experience of widowhood. The findings concerning adaptation suggest that, despite the crisis of widowhood as a particularly stressful life event, most individuals adapt well over time, although the process of reconstruction of a new life and social world is frequently a long and painful one. Many women, in particular, fare well in widowhood and underscore Lopata's (1975) point that widowhood is not necessarily "a state of deprivation or deficit." For many people, widowhood represents a crisis not in the sense of "a threat of catastrophe but rather a turning point, a crucial period of increased vulnerability and heightened potential" (Erikson, as cited in Munnichs and Olbrich 1985, 9). Many realize that potential although, as they advance in age and grow increasingly frail, the threat of becoming dependent looms large in their lives.

Levels of social support for the widowed were found to be uniformly high, in terms of patterns of support and perceptions of the availability of supportive relations. The widowed, in fact, appear to have stronger support networks than do the separated/divorced, despite other similarities in the process of the termination of a marriage.

Extraordinary variability characterizes the experience of widowhood, however. The rural aged have marginally stronger supportive relationships with family and friends, but lack the economic resources and access to transportation available to the urban widowed. Widowers appear comparatively disadvantaged in their ties to family and in their domestic skills, but both these patterns may be cohort-specific. While social policies have been developed to address issues of particular concern to the widowed, social programs will need to be as flexible as possible, because the characteristics of today's widowed elderly — in terms of social roles and expectations, availability of family members, labour force history, education, and financial resources — will be fundamentally different from the attributes of the widowed elderly of tomorrow.

BIBLIOGRAPHY

Adams, D. L.
1975   "Who Are the Rural Aged?" Pp. 11-23 in R.C. Atchley (ed.), *Rural Environments and Aging*. Washington, D.C.: Gerontological Society of America.

Adams, R.
1985   "People Would Talk: Normative Barriers to Cross-Sex Friendships for Elderly Women." *The Gerontologist* 25(6): 605-11.

Aitken, J.
1975   "Guilt is the Enemy, Grief the Friend: Surviving the Death of a Mate." *Weekend Magazine* 25(3).

Allen, K. R.
1989   *Single Women/Family Ties: Life Histories of Older Women*. Newbury Park, Calif.: Sage Publications.

Anderson, T. B.
1984   "Widowhood as a Life Transition: Its Impact on Kinship Ties." *Journal of Marriage and the Family* 46(1): 105-14.
1987   "Widows in Urban Nebraska: Their Informal Support Systems." Pp. 109-35 in H.Z. Lopata (ed.), *Widows*. Vol. 2, *North America*. Durham, N.C.: Duke University Press.

Arens, D. A.
1982   "Widowhood and Well-being: An Examination of Sex Differences within in a Causal Model." *International Journal of Aging and Human Development* 15(1): 27-40.

Arling, G.
1976   "Resistance to Isolation among Elderly Widows." *International Journal of Aging and Human Development* 7(1): 67-86.

Arsenault, A. M.
1986   "Sources of Support of Elderly Acadian Widows." *Health Care for Women International* 7(3): 203-19.

Atchley, R. C.
1972   *The Social Forces in Later Life*. Belmont, Calif.: Wadsworth Publishing Co.
1975   "Dimensions of Widowhood in Later Life." *The Gerontologist* 15(April): 176-78.

Babchuk, N., and T.B. Anderson
1989   "Older Widows and Married Women: Their Intimates and Confidants." *International Journal of Aging and Human Development* 28(1): 21-35.

Balkwell, C.
1981   "Transition to Widowhood: A Review of the Literature." *Family Relations* 30(1): 117-27.

1985   "An Attitudinal Correlate of the Timing of a Major Life Event: The Case of Morale in Widowhood." *Family Relations* 34(3): 577-81.

Ball, J.F.
1977   "Widows' Grief: The Impact of Age and Mode of Death." *Omega: The Journal of Death and Dying* 7:307-33.

Bankoff, E. A.
1983a   "Aged Parents and Their Widowed Daughters: A Support Relationship." *Journal of Gerontology* 38(2): 226-30.

1983b   "Social Support and Adaptation to Widowhood." *Journal of Marriage and the Family* 45(4): 826-39.

1986   "Peer Support for Widows: Personal and Structural Characteristics Related to Its Provision." Pp. 207-22 in S. E. Hobfall (ed.) *Stress, Social Support and Women*. Washington, D.C.: Hemisphere Publishing.

Barrett, C. J.
1978   "Sex Differences in the Experiences of Widowhood." Paper presented at the American Psychological Association Annual Meeting, Toronto, September.

Barrett, C. J., and K. M. Schneweis
1980 - "An Empirical Search for Stages of Widowhood." *Omega: The Journal of*
1981   *Death and Dying* 11(2): 97-104.

Becker, H. S.
1970   *Sociological Work: Method and Substance*. Chicago: Aldine Publishing Company.

Bensel-Meyers, L. D.
1985   "A 'Figure Cut in Alabaster'": The Paradoxical Widow of Renaissance Drama." Ph.D. dissertation, Department of English, University of Oregon.

Berardo, F. M.
1970   "Survivorship and Social Isolation: The Case of the Aged Widower." *Family Co-ordinator* 19:11-15.

1985   "Social Networks and Life Preservation." *Death Studies* 9:37-50.

Berger, P. L., and H. Kellner
1970   "Marriage and the Construction of Reality." Pp. 49-72 in H. P. Drietzel (ed.), *Recent Sociology*. No. 2. New York: Macmillan.

Berger, P. L., B. Berger, and H. Kellner
1973   *The Homeless Mind: Modernization and Consciousness*. New York: Vintage Books.

Blanchard, C. G., E. B. Blanchard, and J. N. Becker
1976   "The Young Widow: Depressive Symptomatology throughout the Grief Process." *Psychiatry* 39: 394-99.

Blau, Z. S.
1973   *Old Age in a Changing Society*. New York: New Viewpoints.

Blishen, B., W. K. Carroll, and C. Moore
1987   "The 1981 Socio-economic Index for Occupations in Canada." *Canadian Review of Sociology and Anthropology* 24(4): 465-88.

Blumer, H.
1969   *Symbolic Interactionism: Perspective and Method*. Englewood Cliffs, N.J.: Prentice-Hall.

Bock, E. W., and I. L. Webber
   1972   "Suicide among the Elderly: Isolating Widowhood and Mitigating Alternatives." *Journal of Marriage and the Family* 34:24-31.
Bohm, L. C., and J. Rodin
   1985   "Aging and the Family." Pp. 279-310 in D.C. Turk and R.D. Kerns (eds.), *Health, Illness and Families: A Life-Span Perspective*. New York: John Wiley & Sons.
Bowling, A., and A. Cartwright
   1982   *Life after a Death*. London: Tavistock.
Browning, K. F., and J. B. Bond, Jr.
   1987   "Satisfaction in Retirement." *Canadian Home Economics Journal* 37(1): 18-20.
Caine, L.
   1974   *Widow*. New York: Wm. Morrow and Company.
Canadian Council on Homemaker Services
   1982   *Visiting Homemaker Services in Canada Survey*. Toronto.
   1985   *Homemaker Services in Canada Survey*. Toronto.
Cantor, M. H.
   1979   "Neighbors and Friends: An Overlooked Resource in the Informal Support System." *Research on Aging* 1(4): 434-63.
Cape, E.
   1987   "Aging Women in Rural Settings." Pp. 84-99 in V. W. Marshall (ed.) *Aging in Canada: Social Perspectives* (2d ed.). Toronto: Fitzhenry and Whiteside.
Carey, R. G.
   1979-   "Weathering Widowhood: Problems and Adjustment of the Widowed
   1980   during the First Year." *Omega: The Journal of Death and Dying* 10(2): 163-74.
Caserta, M. S., D. A. Lund, and M. F. Dimond
   1985   "Assessing Interviewer Effects in a Longitudinal Study of Bereaved Elderly Adults." *Journal of Gerontology* 40(5): 637-40.
Chan, K. B.
   1983   "Coping with Aging and Managing Self-Identity: The Social World of the Elderly Chinese Woman." *Canadian Ethnic Studies* 15(3): 36-50.
Chappell, N. L., and L. W. Guse
   1989   "Linkages between Informal and Formal Support." Pp. 219-37 in K. S. Markides and C. L. Cooper (eds.), *Aging, Stress and Health*. Chichester, England: John Wiley and Sons.
Chappell, N. L., L. A. Strain, and A. A. Blandford
   1986   *Aging and Health Care: A Social Perspective*. Toronto: Holt, Rinehart and Winston of Canada.
Christiansen-Ruffman, L.
   1976   "Newcomer Careers: An Exploratory Study of Migrants in Halifax." Ph.D. dissertation, Department of Sociology, Columbia University.
Cicirelli, V. G.
   1980   "Sibling Relationships in Adulthood: Life Span Perspectives." Pp. 455-62 in L.W. Poon (ed.), *Aging in the 1980s: Psychological Issues*. Washington, D.C.: American Psychological Association.

Clark, P. G., R. W. Siviski, and R. Weiner
1986   "Coping Strategies of Widowers in the First Year." *Family Relations* 35(3): 425-30.
Clark, R. L.
1990   "Income Maintenance Policies in the United States." Pp. 382-414 in R. H. Binstock and L. K. George (eds.), *Handbook of Aging and the Social Sciences* (3d ed.). San Diego, Calif.: Academic Press.
Clayton, P. J., J. A. Halikas, W. L. Maurice, and E. Robins
1973   "Anticipatory Grief and Widowhood." *British Journal of Psychiatry* 122: 47-51.
Cobb, S.
1976   "Social Support as a Moderator of Life Stress." *Psychosomatic Medicine* 38: 300-14.
Cohen, S., R. Mermelstein, T. Kamarck, and H. Hoberman
1984   "Measuring the Functional Components of Social Support." Pp. 73-94 in I. Sarason (ed.), *Social Support: Theory, Research and Applications*. The Hague: Martines Niijhoff.
Cohen, S., and S. L. Syme (eds.)
1985   *Social Support and Health*. New York: Academic Press.
Colsher, P. L., and R. B. Wallace
1990   "Health and Social Antecedents of Relocation in Rural Elderly Persons." *Journal of Gerontology: Social Sciences* 45(1): S32-38.
Connidis, I. A.
1982   "Women and Retirement: The Effect of Multiple Careers on Retirement Adjustment." *Canadian Journal on Aging* 1:17-27.
1989a   "Siblings as Friends in Later Life." *American Behavioral Scientist* 33(1): 81-93.
1989b   *Family Ties and Aging*. Toronto: Butterworths.
1989c   "Contact between Siblings in Later Life." *Canadian Journal of Sociology* 14(4): 429-42.
Cooney, T. M.
1989   "Co-residence with Adult Children: A Comparison of Divorced and Widowed Women." *The Gerontologist* 29(6): 779-84.
Coward, R. T.
1987   "Factors Associated with the Helping Networks of Noninstitutionalized Elders." *Journal of Gerontological Social Work* 10(1/2): 113-32.
Cumming, E., and W. E. Henry
1961   *Growing Old: The Process of Disengagement*. New York: Basic Books.
Cunningham, G. E.
1988   "Health Status and Coping among Elderly Rural Widows: Residential Differences." Unpublished M.H.S. thesis, Faculty of Health Sciences, McMaster University, Hamilton, Ontario.
Cusack, S. A.
1988   *The W.H.O. C.A.N. Experience: An Evaluation Report of Widows' Support Groups in British Columbia and Their First Provincial Conference*. Report to New Horizons of Canada, June.
David, M., and J. Fitzgerald
1988   *Survey of Income and Program Participation: Measuring Poverty and Crises*.

U.S. Department of Health and Human Services: Survey of Income and Program Participation, Working Paper No. 8805, July.

Demi, A. S.
1989 "Death of a Spouse." Pp. 218-48 in R. A. Kalish (ed.), *Midlife Loss: Coping Strategies*. Newbury Park, Calif.: Sage Publications.

Devereaux, M. S.
1988 "1986 Census Highlights: Marital Status." Pp. 24-27 in Statistics Canada, *Canadian Social Trends*. Ottawa: Minister of Supply and Services Canada.

DiGiulio, R. C.
1989 *Beyond Widowhood*. New York: Free Press.

Dorfman, L. T., and M. M. Moffet
1987 "Retirement Satisfaction in Married and Widowed Rural Women." *The Gerontologist* 27(2): 215-21.

Driedger, L., and N. Chappell
1987 *Aging and Ethnicity: Toward an Interface*. Toronto: Butterworths.

Dulude, L.
1979 *Women and Aging: A Report on the Rest of our Lives*. Ottawa: Advisory Council on the Status of Women.

Elias, B.
1977 "Residential Environment and Social Adjustment among Older Widows." Unpublished M.Sc. thesis, Department of Family Studies, University of Guelph.

Elwell, F., and A. D. Maltbie
1978 "Differential Effects of Widowhood: Two Models and Empirical Tests." Paper presented at the annual meeting of the Gerontological Society of America, Dallas.

Erikson, E.
1968 *Identity, Youth and Crisis*. New York: W.W. Norton Co.

Evans, J.
1971 *Living with a Man Who Is Dying: A Personal Memoir*. New York: Taplinger Publishing Company.

Fengler, A. P., and N. Danigelis
1982 "Residence, the Elderly Widow, and Life Satisfaction." *Research on Aging* 4(1): 113-15.

Fengler, A. P., and R. Goodrich
1979 "Wives of Elderly Disabled Men: The Hidden Patients." *The Gerontologist* 19(2): 175-83.

Fenwick, R., and C. M. Barresi
1981 "Health Consequences of Marital-Status Change among the Elderly: A Comparison of Cross-sectional and Longitudinal Analyses." *Journal of Health and Social Behaviour* 22(2): 106-16.

Ferraro, K. F.
1985- "The Effect of Widowhood on the Health Status of Older Persons."
1986 *International Journal of Aging and Human Development* 21(1): 9-25.
1989 "Widowhood and Health." Pp. 69-89 in K. S. Markides and C. L. Cooper (eds.), *Aging, Stress and Health*. Chichester, England: John Wiley and Sons.

Ferraro, K. F., and C. M. Barresi
1982 "The Impact of Widowhood on the Social Relations of Older Persons." *Research on Aging* 4(2): 227-47.

Ferraro, K. F., E. Mutran, and C. M. Barresi
1984 "Widowhood, Health, and Friendship Support in Later Life." *Journal of Health and Social Behaviour* 25(3): 246-59.

Fletcher, S., and L. O. Stone
1980 "The Living Arrangements of Older Women." *Essence: Issues in the Study of Ageing, Dying and Death* 4(3): 115-33.

Fooken, I.
1985 "Old and Female: Psychosocial Concomitants of the Aging Process in a Group of Older Women." Pp. 77-101 in J. Munnichs, P. Mussen, E. Olbrich, and P. G. Coleman (eds.) *Life-Span and Change in a Gerontological Perspective*. Orlando, Fla.: Academic Press.

Forbes, W. F., J. A. Jackson, and A. S. Kraus
1987 *Institutionalization of the Elderly in Canada*. Toronto: Butterworths.

Gallagher, D., S. Lovett, P. Hanley-Dunn, and L. W. Thompson
1989 "Use of Select Coping Strategies during Late-Life Spousal Bereavement." Pp. 111-21 in D. A. Lund (ed.), *Older Bereaved Spouses: Research with Practical Applications*. New York: Hemisphere Publishing.

Gee, E. M.
1986 "The Life Course of Canadian Women: An Historical and Demographic Analysis." *Social Indicators Research* 18:263-83.

Gee, E. M., and M. M. Kimball
1987 *Women and Aging*. Toronto: Butterworths.

Gentry, M., and A. D. Shulman
1985 "Survey of Sampling Techniques in Widowhood Research, 1973-1983." *Journal of Gerontology* 40(5): 641-43.
1988 "Remarriage as a Coping Response for Widowhood." *Psychology and Aging* 3(2): 191-96.

Gerber, I., R. Rusalem, N. Hannon, D. Battin, and A. Arkin
1975 "Anticipatory Grief and Aged Widows and Widowers." *Journal of Gerontology* 30:225-29.

Gibbs, J. M.
1980 "The Social World of the Older Widow in the Non-Metropolitan Community." Ph.D. dissertation, Department of Sociology, Anthropology and Social Work, Kansas State University, Manhattan, Kansas.
1985 "Family Relations of the Older Widow: Their Location and Importance for Her Social Life." Pp. 91-104 in W. A. Peterson and J. Quadagno (eds.), *Social Bonds in Later Life: Aging and Interdependence*. Beverly Hills, Calif.: Sage Publications.

Glaser, B., and A. L. Strauss
1971 *Status Passage: A Formal Theory*. Chicago: Aldine-Atherton.

Glick, I. O., S. Weiss, and C. M. Parkes
1974 *The First Year of Bereavement*. New York: John Wiley & Sons.

Gnaedinger, N. J.
1986 "Elderly Widows Who Live Alone in Their Own Houses: Assessments of Risk." M.A. thesis, Institute of Canadian Studies, Carleton University, Ottawa.

Gottlieb, B. H.
  1981 "Social Networks and Social Support in Community Mental Health."
        Pp. 11-42 in B. H. Gottlieb (ed.), *Social Networks and Social Support*. Beverly
        Hills, Calif.: Sage Publications.
Gove, W. R.
  1973 "Sex, Marital Status and Mortality." *American Journal of Sociology* 79:45-
        67.
Gove, W. R., and H.-C. Shin
  1989 "The Psychological Well-being of Divorced and Widowed Men and
        Women." *Journal of Family Issues* 10(1): 122-44.
Government of Canada
  1979 *Retirement without Tears: The Report of the Special Senate Committee on
        Retirement Age Policies*. Ottawa: Minister of Supply and Services Canada.
  1982 *The Charter of Rights and Freedoms: A Guide for Canadians*. Ottawa: Min-
        ister of Supply and Services.
Government of the Province of Alberta
  1983 *Widows' Pension Act*: Chapter W-7.5. 1983. Edmonton: Queen's Printer.
Graham, K., A. Zeidman, M. C. Flower, S. J. Saunders, and M. White-Campbell.
  1989 *Case Study Analyses of Elderly Persons Who Have Alcohol Problems*. Final
        Report to NHRDP, Project No. 6606-3414-43DA. Ottawa: Health and
        Welfare Canada.
Granovetter, M. S.
  1973 "The Strength of Weak Ties." *American Journal of Sociology* 78(6):1360-80.
Greene, R. W., and S. Feld
  1989 "Social Support Coverage and the Well-being of Elderly Widows and
        Married Women." *Journal of Family Issues* 10(1):33-51.
Haas-Hawkings, G.
  1978 "Intimacy as a Moderating Influence on the Stress of Loneliness in
        Widowhood." *Essence: Issues in the Study of Ageing, Dying and Death* 2(4):
        249-58.
Haas-Hawkings, G., S. Sangster, M. Ziegler, and D. Reid
  1985 "A Study of Relatively Immediate Adjustment to Widowhood in Later
        Life." *International Journal of Women's Studies* 8(2): 158-66.
Hagestad, G. O.
  1981 "Problems and Promises in the Social Psychology of Intergenerational
        Relations." Pp. 11-46 in R. W. Fogel, E. Hatfield, S. B. Kiesler, and E.
        Shanas (eds.), *Aging: Stability and Change in the Family*. New York:
        Academic Press.
  1988 "Demographic Change and the Life Course: Some Emerging Trends in
        the Family Realm." *Family Relations* 37(4): 405-10.
Harbert, A., and C. Wilkinson
  1979 "Growing Old in Rural America." *Aging* 291: 36-40.
Harris, M., and C. D. Harvey
  1987 "Information Received for Decisions Made by Widows." *International
        Journal of Sociology of the Family* 17(2): 227-38.
Hartwigsen, G.
  1987 "Older Widows and the Transference of Home." *International Journal of
        Aging and Human Development* 25(3): 195-207.

Harvey, C. D., and H. M. Bahr
  1974 "Widowhood, Morale, and Affiliation." *Journal of Marriage and the Family* 36:97-106.
  1980 *The Sunshine Widows: Adapting to Sudden Bereavement.* Lexington, Mass.: Lexington Books.
Harvey, C.D., G. E. Barnes, and L. Greenwood
  1987 "Correlates of Morale among Canadian Widowed Persons." *Social Psychiatry* 22 (2): 65–72.
Harvey, C. D., and M. Harris
  1985 "Decision-Making during Widowhood: The Beginning Years." Paper presented at the Beatrice Paolucci Symposium, Michigan State University, July 19.
Harvey, C. D., G. E. Barnes, L. J. Greenwood, and R. Kabahenda-Nyakabwa
  1987 "Activities, Religiosity, and Morale of Canadian Widowed Persons." Pp. 251-72 in H. Z. Lopata (ed.), *Widows.* Vol. 2, *North America.* Durham, N.C.: Duke University Press.
Health and Welfare Canada
  1982 *Pension Plan Coverage by Level of Earnings and Age 1978 and 1979.* Ottawa: Planning, Evaluation and Liaison Division, Income Security Programs Branch.
  1983 *Fact Book on Aging in Canada.* Ottawa: Minister of Supply and Services.
Helsing, K., and M. Szklo
  1981 "Mortality after Bereavement." *American Journal of Epidemiology* 144 (July): 42-52.
Hennon, C. B.
  1983 "Divorce and the Elderly: A Neglected Area of Research." Pp. 149-72 in T. H. Brubaker (ed.), *Family Relationships in Later Life.* Beverly Hills, Calif.: Sage Publications.
Heyman, D., and D. Gianturco
  1973 "Long-Term Adaptation of the Elderly to Bereavement." *Journal of Gerontology* 28(4): 359-62.
Hill, C. D., L. W. Thompson, and D. Gallagher
  1988 "The Role of Anticipatory Bereavement in Older Women's Adjustment to Widowhood." *The Gerontologist* 28(6): 792-96.
Himmelfarb, A., and C. J. Richardson
  1982 *Sociology for Canadians: Images of Society.* Toronto: McGraw-Hill Ryerson.
Holden, K. C., R. B. Burkhauser, and D. A. Myers
  1986 "Income Transitions at Older Stages of Life: The Dynamics of Poverty." *The Gerontologist* 26(3): 292-97.
Holmes, T. H., and R. H. Rahe
  1967 "The Social Readjustment Rating Scale." *Journal of Psychosomatic Research* 11(2): 213-18.
Horowitz, A.
  1985 "Sons and Daughters as Caregivers to Older Parents: Differences in Role Performance and Consequences." *The Gerontologist* 25(6): 612-17.
House, J. S., and R. L. Kahn
  1985 "Measures and Concepts of Social Support." Pp. 83-108 in S. Cohen and S. L. Syme (eds.), *Social Support and Health.* New York: Academic Press.

Hudson, C. M.
  1984   "The Transition from Wife to Widow: Short-Term Changes in Economic
          Well-being and Labor Force Behavior." Ph.D. dissertation, Department
          of Sociology, Duke University, Durham, N.C.
Hurd, M. D.
  1987   *The Poverty of Widows: Future Prospects.* NBER Working Paper No. 2326.
          Cambridge, Mass.: National Bureau of Economic Research.
Hurd, M. D. and D. A. Wise
  1987   *The Wealth and Poverty of Widows: Assets before and after the Husband's
          Death.* Working Paper No. 2325. Cambridge, Mass.: National Bureau of
          Economic Research.
Hyman, H. H.
  1983   *Of Time and Widowhood.* Duke Press Policy Studies, Durham, N.C.
Income Security Programs
  1987a   *Your Old Age Security Pension.* Ottawa: Minister of Supply and Services
          Canada.
  1987b   *Your Spouse's Allowance.* Ottawa: Minister of Supply and Services
          Canada.
Ingebretsen, R.
  1986   "Widow(er)s' Experience of Closeness to Their Deceased Spouses." Pp.
          171-72 in *Congress Proceedings,* 8th Scandinavian Congress of Geronto-
          logy, Tampere.
Kaplan, B. H., J. C. Cassel, and S. Gore
  1977   "Social Support and Health." *Medical Care* 15(Suppl. 5): 47-58.
Kendig, H. L.
  1990   "Comparative Perspectives on Housing, Aging and Social Structure."
          Pp. 288-306 in R. H. Binstock and L. K. George (eds.), *Handbook of Aging
          and the Social Sciences* (3d ed.). San Diego, Calif.: Academic Press.
Kestenbaum, B., and G. Diez
  1982   "Mortality of Older Widows and Wives." *Social Security Bulletin* 45(10):
          24-27.
Kitson, G. C., H. Z. Lopata, W. M. Holmes, and S. M. Meyering
  1980   "Divorcees and Widows: Similarities and Differences." *American Jour-
          nal of Orthopsychiatry* 50:291-301.
Kitson, G. C., K. Benson Babri, M. I. Roach, and K. S. Placidi
  1989   "Adjustment to Widowhood and Divorce: A Review." *Journal of Family
          Issues* 10(1): 5-32.
Knudsen, N. K.
  1988   "Cross-Sex Friendships in Later Life." M.Sc. thesis, Department of
          Family Studies, University of Guelph, Guelph, Ontario.
Kohn, J. B., and W. K. Kohn
  1978   *The Widower.* Boston: Beacon Press.
Kraus, A. S.
  1976   "Elderly Applicants to Long-Term Care Institutions: I. Their Character-
          istics, Health Problems, and State of Mind." *Journal of the American Ge-
          riatrics Society* 24(3): 117-25.
Krout, J. A.
  1986   *The Aged in Rural America.* New York: Greenwood Press.

Kulys, R., and S. S. Tobin
  1980   "Older People and Their Responsible Others." *Social Work* March: 138-
          45.
Lassey, W. R., M. L. Lassey, G. R. Lee, and N. Lee (eds.)
  1980   *Research and Public Service with the Rural Elderly: Proceedings of a Confer-
          ence.* Publication No. 4. Corvallis, Oregon: Western Rural Development
          Center, Oregon State University.
Lawton, M. P.
  1972   "The Dimensions of Morale." Pp. 152-53 in D. Kent, R. Kastenbaum, and
          S. Sherwood (eds.), *Research Planning and Action for the Elderly.* New York:
          Behavioral Publications.
Lee, G. R., and Cassidy, M. L.
  1985   "Family and Kin Relations of the Rural Elderly." Pp. 151-69 in R. T.
          Coward and G. R. Lee (eds.), *The Elderly in Rural Society.* New York:
          Springer Publishing Co.
Lehman, D. R., C. B. Wortman, and A. F. Williams
  1987   "Long-Term Effects of Losing a Spouse or Child in a Motor Vehicle
          Crash." *Journal of Personality and Social Psychology* 52(1): 218-31.
Lieberman, M. A., and L. Videka-Sherman
  1986   "The Impact of Self-Help Groups on the Mental Health of Widows and
          Widowers." *American Journal of Orthopsychiatry* 56(3): 435-49.
Livingstone, B.
  1988   "Separated and Unequal: Divorcees Seek Widows' Pensions." *Hamilton
          Spectator* February 16.
Longino, C. F., Jr.
  1990   "Geographic Distribution and Migration." Pp. 45-63 in R. H. Binstock
          and L. K. George (eds.), *Handbook of Aging and the Social Sciences* (3d ed.).
          San Diego, Calif.: Academic Press.
Lopata, H.Z.
  1973a   "Self-Identity in Marriage and Widowhood." *Sociological Quarterly*
          14(3): 407-18.
  1973b   *Widowhood in an American City.* Cambridge, Mass.: Schenkman.
  1975   "Widowhood: Societal Factors in Life-span Disruptions and Alterna-
          tives." Pp. 217-34 in N. Datan and L. H. Ginsberg (eds.), *Life-span De-
          velopmental Psychology: Normative Life Crises.* New York: Academic Press.
  1978   "Contributions of Extended Families to the Support Systems of Metro-
          politan Area Widows: Limitations of the Modified Kin Network."
          Journal of Marriage and the Family 40(2): 355-64.
  1979   *Women as Widows: Support Systems.* New York: Elsevier.
  1981   "Widowhood and Husband Sanctification." *Journal of Marriage and the
          Family* 43(2): 439-50.
  1987a   *Widows.* Vol. 1, *The Middle East, Asia, and the Pacific.* Durham, N.C.: Duke
          University Press.
  1987b   *Widows.* Vol. 2, *North America.* Durham, N.C.: Duke University Press.
Lowenthal, M. F., and C. Haven
  1968   "Interaction and Adaptation: Intimacy as a Critical Variable." Pp. 390-
          400 in B. Neugarten (ed.), *Middle Age and Aging.* Chicago: University of
          Chicago Press.

Lubben, J. E.
  1988 "Gender Differences in the Relationship of Widowhood and Psychological Well-being among Low Income Elderly." *Women and Health* 14(3/4): 161-89.
Lund, D. A. (ed.)
  1989a "Conclusions about Bereavement in Later Life and Implications for Interventions and Future Research." Pp. 217-31 in D. A. Lund (ed.) *Older Bereaved Spouses: Research with Practical Applications*. New York: Hemisphere Publishing.
  1989b *Older Bereaved Spouses: Research with Practical Implications*. New York: Hemisphere Publishing.
Lund, D. A., M. Dimond, M. Caserta, R. Johnson, J. Poulton, and R. Connelly
  1985- "Identifying Elderly with Coping Difficulties after Two Years of Be-
  1986   reavement." *Omega: The Journal of Death and Dying* 16(3): 210-19.
Lund, D. A., D. E. Redburn, M. S. Juretich, and M. S. Caserta
  1989 "Resolving Problems Implementing Bereavement Self-Help Groups." Pp. 203-16 in D. A. Lund (ed.), *Older Bereaved Spouses: Research with Practical Applications*. New York: Hemisphere Publishing.
MacRae, H. M.
  1987 "Identity and Its Maintenance in Later Life: A Social Network Approach." Ph.D. dissertation, Department of Sociology, McMaster University, Hamilton, Ontario.
Maddison, D., and W. L. Walker
  1967 "Factors Affecting the Outcome of Conjugal Bereavement." *British Journal of Psychiatry* 113:1057-67.
Markides, K. S., and C. L. Cooper
  1989 "Aging, Stress, Social Support and Health: An Overview." Pp. 1-10 in K. S. Markides and C. L. Cooper (eds.), *Aging, Stress and Health*. Chichester, England: John Wiley and Sons.
Marris, P.
  1958 *Widows and Their Families*. London: Routledge and Kegan Paul.
Marshall, V.W.
  1981 "Social Characteristics of the Future Aged." Hamilton, Ont.: Program for Quantitative Studies in Economies and Population, McMaster University.
Martin Matthews, A.
  1980a "Wives' Experiences of Relocation: Status Passage and the Moving Career." Ph.D. dissertation, Department of Sociology, McMaster University, Hamilton, Ontario.
  1980b "Women and Widowhood." Pp. 145-53 in V. W. Marshall (ed.), *Aging in Canada: Social Perspectives*. Toronto: Fitzhenry and Whiteside.
  1982 "Canadian Research on Women as Widows: A Comparative Analysis of the State of the Art." *Resources for Feminist Research* 11(2): 227-30.
  1987a "Widowhood as an Expectable Life Event." Pp. 343-66 in V. W. Marshall (ed.), *Aging in Canada: Social Perspectives* (2d ed.). Toronto: Fitzhenry and Whiteside.
  1987b "Support Systems of Widows in Canada." Pp. 225-50 in H. Z. Lopata (ed.), *Widows*. Vol. 2, *North America*. Durham, N.C.: Duke University Press.

1988a   "Social Supports of the Rural Widowed Elderly." *Journal of Rural Health* 4(3): 57-70.

1988b   "Variations in the Conceptualization and Measurement of Rurality: Conflicting Findings on the Elderly Widowed." *Journal of Rural Studies* 4(2): 141-50.

Martin Matthews, A., and K. H. Brown
1987   "Retirement as a Critical Life Event: The Differential Experiences of Women and Men." *Research on Aging* 19(4): 548-71.

Martin Matthews, A., and J. A. Tindale
1987   "Retirement in Canada." Pp. 43-75 in K. S. Markides and C. L. Cooper (eds.), *Retirement in Industrialized Societies: Social, Psychological and Health Factors*. Sussex: John Wiley and Sons.

Martin Matthews, A., K. H. Brown, C. K. Davis, and M. A. Denton
1982   "A Crisis Assessment Technique for the Evaluation of Life Events: Transition to Retirement as an Example." *Canadian Journal on Aging* 1(3/4): 28-39.

Matthews, S. H.
1986   *Friendships through the Life Course: Oral Biographies in Old Age*. Beverly Hills, Calif.: Sage Publications.

McCall, G. J., and J. L. Simmons
1966   *Identities and Interactions*. New York: Free Press.

McCallum, J.
1986   "Retirement and Widowhood Transitions." Pp. 129-48 in H. L. Kendig (ed.), *Ageing and Families: A Social Support Networks Perspective*. Sydney: Allen and Unwin.

McCallum, J., and B. Shadbolt
1989   "Ethnicity and Stress among Older Australians." *Journal of Gerontology: Social Sciences* 44(3): S89-S96.

McCourt, W. F., R. D. Barnett, J. Brennan, and A. Becker
1976   "We Help Each Other: Primary Prevention for the Widowed." *American Journal of Psychiatry* 133(1): 98-100.

McCracken, G.
1988   "Lois Roget: Curatorial Consumer in a Modern Society." Pp. 44-53 in G. McCracken, *Culture and Consumption: New Approaches to the Symbolism of Consumer Goods and Activities*. Bloomington: Indiana University Press.

McDaniel, S. A.
1986   *Canada's Aging Population*. Toronto: Butterworths.

McFarlane, A. H., G. R. Norman, D. L. Streiner, R. Roy, and D. J. Scott
1980   "A Longitudinal Study of Influence of the Psycho-social Environment on Health Status: A Preliminary Report." *Journal of Health and Social Behaviour* 21:124-33.

McGloshen, T. H., and S. L. O'Bryant
1988   "The Psychological Well-being of Older, Recent Widows." *Psychology of Women Quarterly* 12:99-116.

McLaren, S.
1990   Personal communication, Calgary Widowed Services, Calgary, Alberta, March 13.

Mead, G. H.
1964   *On Social Psychology: Selected Papers.* Chicago: University of Chicago Press.
Mills, C. W.
1959   *The Sociological Imagination.* New York: Grove Press.
Moody, H. R.
1985   "Self-Help and Mutual-Aid for Older People." *Aging* 349:31-35.
Morgan, D. L.
1989   "Social Networks and the Adjustment to Widowhood: Patterns of Commitment and Flexibility." *The Gerontologist* 29(1): 101-7.
Morgan, L. A.
1976   "A Re-examination of Widowhood and Morale." *Journal of Gerontology* 31(6): 687-95.
1981   "Economic Change at Mid-life Widowhood: A Longitudinal Analysis." *Journal of Marriage and the Family* 43(4): 899-907.
1983   "Intergenerational Economic Assistance to Children: The Case of Widows and Widowers." *Journal of Gerontology* 38(6): 725-31.
1986   "The Financial Experience of Widowed Women: Evidence from the LRHS." *The Gerontologist* 26(6): 663-68.
1987   "Gender and Poverty among the Widowed: A Comment on Smith and Zick." *Journal of Marriage and the Family* 49(4): 689-94.
1989   "Economic Well-being Following Marital Termination." *Journal of Family Issues* 10(1): 86-101.
Munnichs, J. M. A., and E. Olbrich
1985   "Life-span and Change in a Gerontological Perspective." Pp. 3-11 in J. M. A. Munnichs, P. Mussen, E. Olbrich, and P. G. Coleman (eds.), *Life-span and Change in a Gerontological Perspective.* Orlando, Fla.: Academic Press.
Nagy, M. C.
1982   "Attributional Differences in Health Status and Life Satisfaction of Older Women: A Comparison between Widows and Non-Widows." Ph.D. dissertation, Department of Health Education, University of Oregon.
National Council of Welfare
1984   *Sixty-Five and Older: A Report by the National Council of Welfare on the Incomes of the Aged.* Ottawa: Minister of Supply and Services.
1988   *Poverty Profile 1988: A Report by the National Council of Welfare.* Ottawa: Minister of Supply and Services.
Neugarten, B. L., and G. O. Hagestad
1976   "Age and the Life Course." Pp. 35-55 in E. Shanas and R. Binstock (eds.), *Handbook of Aging and the Social Sciences.* New York: Van Nostrand Reinhold.
Norris, J. E.
1980   "The Social Adjustment of Single and Widowed Older Women." *Essence: Issues in the Study of Ageing, Dying and Death* 4(3): 135-44.
Northcott, H. C.
1984   "Widowhood and Remarriage Trends in Canada 1956-1981." *Canadian Journal on Aging* 3(2): 63-78.

O'Brien, R. A.
  1987   *Social Support Processes in Well-Being of Bereaved*. Final Report # AG04028 to the Behavioural and Social Research Program, U.S. National Institute on Aging, Department of Health and Human Services, Washington, D.C.
O'Bryant, S. L.
  1982   "The Value of Home to Older Persons and Its Relationship to Housing Satisfaction." *Research on Aging* 4:349-63.
  1987   "Attachment to Home and Support Systems of Older Widows in Columbus, Ohio." Pp. 48-70 in H. Z. Lopata (ed.), *Widows*. Vol. 2, *North America*. Durham, N.C.: Duke University Press.
  1988   "Sibling Support and Older Widows' Well-being." *Journal of Marriage and the Family* 50(1):173-83.
  1989   "Quality of Life for Young-Old and Old-Old Widows." Paper presented at the annual meeting of the Gerontological Society of America, Minneapolis, November 17-21.
  1991   "Forewarning of Husband's Death: Does It Make a Difference?" *Omega: The Journal of Death and Dying*. Forthcoming.
O'Bryant, S. L., and L. A. Morgan
  1989   "Financial Experience and Well-being among Mature Widowed Women." *The Gerontologist* 29(2): 245-51.
  1990   "Recent Widows' Kin Support and Orientations to Self-Sufficiency." *The Gerontologist* 30(3): 391-98.
O'Bryant, S. L., and C. I. Murray
  1986   "'Attachment to Home' and Other Factors Related to Widows' Relocation Decisions." *Journal of Housing for the Elderly* 4(1): 53-72.
O'Bryant, S. L., and L. B. Straw
  1991   "Relationship of Previous Divorce and Previous Widowhood to Older Women's Adjustment to Recent Widowhood." *The Journal of Divorce and Remarriage* 15(3/4). Forthcoming.
Parkes, C. M.
  1970   "The First Year of Bereavement." *Psychiatry* 33:444-67.
  1986   *Bereavement: Studies of Grief in Adult Life*. 2d ed. Harmondsworth, England: Penguin Books.
Parkes, C. M., B. Benjamin, and R. G. Fitzgerald
  1969   "Broken Heart: A Statistical Study of Increased Mortality among Widowers." *British Medical Journal* 1:740-43.
Parliamentary Task Force on Pension Reform
  1983   *Final Report*. Ottawa: Minister of Supply and Services Canada.
Pearlin, L. I.
  1980   "The Life Cycle and Life Strains." Pp. 349-60 in H. M. Blalock, Jr. (ed.), *Sociological Theory and Research: A Critical Approach*. New York: Free Press.
Permaul, J.
  1990   Personal communication, "Widowers Surviving" Project, Sunnybrook Medical Centre, Toronto, April 2.
Peters, G. R., D. R. Hoyt, N. Babchuk, M. Kaiser, and Y. Iljima
  1987   "Primary Group Support Systems of the Aged." *Research on Aging* 9(3): 392-416.

Pihlblad, C. T., D. L. Adams, and D. L. Rosencranz
    1972   "Socio-economic Adjustment to Widowhood." *Omega: The Journal of Death and Dying* 3:295-305.
Pilisuk, M., and M. Minkler
    1980   "Supportive Networks: Life Ties for the Elderly." *Journal of Social Issues* 36(2): 95-116.
Pratt, C. C., L. L. Jones, H. -Y. Skin, and A. J. Walker
    1989   "Autonomy and Decision Making between Single Older Women and Their Caregiving Daughters." *The Gerontologist* 29(6): 792-97.
Rempel, J.
    1985   "Childless Elderly: What Are They Missing?" *Journal of Marriage and the Family* 47(2): 343-48.
Rico-Velasco, J., and L. Mynko
    1973   "Suicide and Marital Status: A Changing Relationship?" *Journal of Marriage and the Family* 35:239-44.
Roach, M. J., and G. C. Kitson
    1989   "Impact of Forewarning on Adjustment to Widowhood and Divorce." Pp. 185-200 in D. A. Lund (ed.), *Older Bereaved Spouses: Research with Practical Applications.* New York: Hemisphere Publishing.
Roadburg, A.
    1985   *Aging: Retirement, Leisure and Work in Canada.* Toronto: Methuen.
Roberto, K. A., and J. P. Scott
    1983   "Between Friends: Patterns of Social Involvement and Mutual Assistance of the Rural Elderly." Paper presented at the Annual Meeting of the Gerontological Society of America, San Francisco.
Robertson, N.C.
    1974   "The Relationship between Marital Status and the Risk of Psychiatric Referral." *British Journal of Psychiatry* 124:191-202.
Robson, K. S.
    1974   "Clinical Report: Letters to a Dead Husband." *Journal of Geriatric Psychiatry* 7(2): 208-32.
Rogers, A.
    1988   "Age Patterns of Elderly Migration: An International Comparison." *Demography* 25:355-70.
Rogers, J., M. L. S. Vachon, W. A. Lyall, A. Sheldon, and S. J. J. Freeman
    1980   "A Self-Help Program for Widows as an Independent Community Service." *Hospital and Community Psychiatry* 31(2): 844-47.
Rosenman, L., and A. D. Shulman
    1987   "Widowed Women in Melbourne, Australia." In H. Z. Lopata (ed.) *Widows.* Vol. 1, *The Middle East, Asia, and the Pacific.* Durham, N.C.: Duke University Press.
Rosenman, L., A. D. Shulman, and R. Penman
    1981   "Support Systems of Widowed Women in Australia." *Australian Journal of Social Issues* 16(1): 18-31.
Rosenthal, C. J.
    1987   "Aging and Generational Relations in Canada." Pp. 311-42 in V. W. Marshall (ed.), *Aging in Canada: Social Perspectives* (2d ed.). Markham, Ont.: Fitzhenry and Whiteside.

Rosenthal, C. J., and P. Dawson
   n.d.   "Families and the Institutionalized Elderly." Forthcoming in G. Jones
           and B. Miesen (eds.), *Caregiving and Dementia: Convergence of Research
           Models and Empirical Reflections*. London: Routledge.
Ross, H. G., and J. I. Milgram
   1982   "Important Variables in Adult Sibling Relationships: A Qualitative
           Study." Pp. 225-49 in M. E. Lamb and B. Sutton-Smith (eds.), *Sibling
           Relationships: Their Nature and Significance across the Lifespan*. Hillsdale,
           N.J.: Lawrence Erlbaum Associates Publishers.
Rubenstein, R. L.
   1986   *Singular Paths: Old Men Living Alone*. New York: Columbia University
           Press.
Saskatchewan Senior Citizens' Provincial Council
   1979   A Report on Widowed Senior Citizens in Regina and Saskatoon. Regina,
           Sask.: The Council.
   1983   *Profile '83: The Senior Populations in Saskatchewan: I Demographics*. Regina,
           Sask.: The Council.
Sawa, R. J.
   1986   "Widowhood." *Canadian Family Physician* 32 (December): 2659-62.
Schlesinger, B.
   1979   *Families: Canada*. Toronto: McGraw-Hill Ryerson.
Schwenger, C. W., and M. J. Gross
   1980   "Institutional Care and Institutionalization of the Elderly in Canada."
           Pp. 248-56 in V. W. Marshall (ed.), *Aging in Canada: Social Perspectives*.
           Toronto: Fitzhenry and Whiteside.
Scott, J. P., and V. R. Kivett
   1985   "Differences in the Morale of Older, Rural Widows and Widowers."
           International Journal of Aging and Human Development 21(2):121-35.
Scott, J. P., and K. A. Roberto
   1985   "Use of Informal and Formal Support Networks by Rural Elderly
           Poor." *The Gerontologist* 25(6): 624-30.
Select Committee on Aging
   1987   *Exploding the Myths: Caregiving in America*. Comm. Pub. No. 99-611, U.S.
           Government Printing Office, Washington, D.C.
Selltiz, C., M. Jahoda, M. Deutsch, and S. W. Cook
   1959   *Research Methods in Social Relations* (rev.). New York: Holt, Rinehart and
           Winston.
Seskin, J.
   1975   *Young Widow*. New York: Ace Books.
Shanas, E., and M. B. Sussman
   1977   *Family, Bureaucracy and the Elderly*. Durham, N.C.: Duke University Press.
Shapiro, E.
   1986   "Patterns and Predictors of Home Care Use by the Elderly When Need
           Is the Sole Basis of Admission." *Home Health Care Services Quarterly* 7(1):
           29-44.
Sheehy, G.
   1976   *Passages: Predictable Crises of Adult Life*. New York: Bantam Books.

Shifrin, L.
  1988   "Widows the Target of Pension Cutbacks." *The Toronto Star*, January 18:
         A15.
Silverman, P. R.
  1986   *Widow-to-Widow*. New York: Springer Publishing Co.
  1987   "Widowhood as the Next Stage in the Life Course." Pp. 170-90 in H. Z.
         Lopata (ed.), *Widows*. Vol. 2, *North America*. Durham, N.C.: Duke Uni-
         versity Press.
Smith, K. R., and C. D. Zick
  1986   "The Incidence of Poverty among the Recently Widowed: Mediating
         Factors in the Life Course." *Journal of Marriage and the Family* 48:619-30.
Smith, W. J.
  1978   "The Etiology of Depression in a Sample of Elderly Widows." *Journal of
         Geriatric Psychiatry* 11(1):81-83.
Statistics Canada
  1982   *Population: Age, Sex and Marital Status*. 1981 Census of Canada, Cata-
         logue No. 92-901. Ottawa: Minister of Supply and Services Canada.
  1983   *Population: Nuptiality and Fertility*. 1981 Census of Canada, Catalogue
         No. 92-906. Ottawa: Minister of Supply and Services Canada.
  1984   *Life Tables, Canada and Provinces 1980-1982*. Catalogue No. 84-532. Ot-
         tawa: Minister of Supply and Services Canada.
  1985a *Vital Statistics* Vol. 2, *Marriages and Divorces*. Catalogue No. 84-205. Ot-
         tawa: Minister of Supply and Services.
  1985b *Women in Canada: A Statistical Report*. Ottawa: Minister of Supply and
         Services Canada.
  1987   *Population: Age, Sex and Marital Status*. 1986 Census of Canada, Cata-
         logue No. 93-901. Ottawa: Minister of Supply and Services, September.
  1988   *Marrying and Divorcing: A Status Report for Canada*. Catalogue No. 89-
         517E. Ottawa: Minister of Supply and Services, September.
  1989   *The Family in Canada: Current Reflections*. Catalogue No. 89-509. Ottawa:
         Minister of Supply and Services.
Stone, L. O.
  1988   *Family and Friendship Ties among Canada's Seniors*. Ottawa: Minister of
         Supply and Services Canada.
Stone, L. O., and S. Fletcher
  1986   *The Seniors Boom*. Ottawa: Statistics Canada.
  1987   "The Hypothesis of Age Patterns in Living Arrangement Passages." Pp.
         288-310 in V. W. Marshall (ed.), *Aging in Canada: Social Perspectives* (2d
         ed.). Toronto: Fitzhenry and Whiteside.
Stone, L. O., and H. Frenken
  1988   *Canada's Seniors*. Catalogue No. 98-121. Ottawa: Minister of Supply and
         Services.
Strain, L. A., and N. L. Chappell
  1982   "Confidants: Do They Make a Difference in Quality of Life?" *Research
         on Aging* 4(4): 479-502.
Strauss, A. L.
  1959   *Mirrors and Masks: The Search for Identity*. Glencoe, Ill.: Free Press.

Stryckman, J.
1981a "Childlessness: Its Impact among the Widowed Elderly." Paper presented to the joint meeting of the Canadian Association on Gerontology and the Gerontological Society of America, Toronto, November.
1981b "The Decision to Remarry: The Choice and Its Outcome." Paper presented at the joint meeting of the Canadian Association on Gerontology and the Gerontological Society of America, Toronto, November.
1982 *Marriages et mises en ménage au cours de la vieillesse.* Université Laval: Laboratoire de gérontologie sociale.

Sudnow, D.
1967 *Passing On: The Social Organization of Dying.* Englewood Cliffs, N.J.: Prentice-Hall.

Synge, J.
1988 "Avoided Conversations: How Parents and Children Delay Talking about Widowhood and Dependency in Later Life." *Ageing and Society* 8(3): 321-35.

Troll, L., S. Miller, and R. C. Atchley
1979 *Families in Later Life.* California: Wadsworth Publishing Co.

Tudiver, F.
1986 "The Bereaved Elderly: Can We Help Them?" *Canadian Family Physician* 32 (December): 2699-2703.
1988 "Elderly Widowers in a Family Practice Setting." *Family Medicine* 20:297-99.

Tudiver, F., J. Hilditch, and J. Permaul
1990 "Factors Associated with Psychosocial Distress of New Widowers." Paper presented at the conference of the North American Primary Care Research Group, Denver, Colorado, May.

Turner, R. H.
1962 "Role-taking: Process versus Conformity." Pp. 20-40 in A.M. Rose (ed.), *Human Behavior and Social Process.* Boston: Houghton Mifflin.

Uhlenberg, P., and M. A. P. Myers
1981 "Divorce and the Elderly." *The Gerontologist* 21(3): 276-82.

Uhlenberg, P., T. Cooney, and R. Boyd
1990 "Divorce for Women after Midlife." *Journal of Gerontology: Social Sciences* 45(1): S3-S11.

Unruh, D.
1983 *Invisible Lives.* Beverly Hills, Calif.: Sage Publications.

Vachon, M. L. S.
1979 "Identity Change over the First Two Years of Bereavement: Social Relationships and Social Support in Widowhood." Ph.D. dissertation, Department of Sociology, York University, Toronto.
1981 "The Importance of Social Relationships and Social Support in Widowhood." Paper presented to the Joint Meeting of the Canadian Association on Gerontology and the Gerontological Society of America, Toronto, November.

Vachon, M. L. S., A. Formo, K. Freedman, A. Lyall, J. Rogers, and S. Freeman
1976 "Stress Reactions to Bereavement." *Essence: Issues in the Study of Ageing, Dying and Death* 1:23-33.

Vachon, M. L. S., K. Freedman, A. Formo, J. Rogers, W. A. Lyall, and S. Freeman
  1977   "The Final Illness in Cancer: The Widow's Perspective." *Canadian Medical Association Journal* 117:1151-54.
Vachon, M. L. S., W.A. Lyall, J. Rogers, K. Freedman-Letofsky, and S. J. J. Freeman
  1980   "A Controlled Study of Self-Help Intervention for Widows." *American Journal of Psychiatry* 137(11): 1380-84.
Vachon, M. L. S., J. Rogers, W. A. Lyall, W. J. Lancee, A. R. Sheldon, and S. J. J. Freeman
  1982   "Predictors and Correlates of Adaptation to Conjugal Bereavement." *American Journal of Psychiatry* 139(8): 998-1002.
Vachon, M. L., A. R. Sheldon, W. J. Lancee, W. A. Lyall, J. Rogers, and S. J. Freeman
  1982   "Correlates of Enduring Distress Patterns Following Bereavement: Social Network, Life Situation and Personality." *Psychological Medicine* 12(4): 783-88.
Vachon, M. L. S., and S. K. Stylianos
  1988   "The Role of Social Support in Bereavement." *Journal of Social Issues* 44(3): 175-90.
Vincente, L., J. Wiley, and A. Carrington
  1979   "The Risk of Institutionalization before Death." *The Gerontologist* 19(4): 361-67.
Walker, K. N., A. MacBride, and M. L. S. Vachon
  1977   "Social Support Networks and the Crisis of Bereavement." *Social Science and Medicine* 11:35-41.
Wan, T. H.
  1982   *Stressful Life Events, Social Support Networks, and Gerontological Health.* Lexington, Mass.: Lexington Books.
  1985   *Well-being for the Elderly: Primary Preventive Strategies.* Lexington, Mass.: Lexington Books.
Willis, L., P. Thomas, P.J. Garry, and J. Goodwin
  1987   "A Prospective Study of Response to Stressful Life Events in Initially Healthy Elders." *Journal of Gerontology* 42(6): 627-30.
Wister, A. V., and L. A. Strain
  1986   "Social Support and Well-being: A Comparison of Older Widows and Widowers." *Canadian Journal on Aging* 5(3): 205-20.
Wortman, C. B., and R. C. Silver
  1990   "Successful Mastery of Bereavement and Widowhood: A Life-Course Perspective." Pp. 225-64 in P. B. Baltes and M. M. Baltes (eds.), *Successful Aging: Perspectives from the Behavioral Sciences.* New York: Cambridge University Press.
Young, M., B. Benjamin, and C. Wallis
  1963   "The Mortality of Widowers." *Lancet* 2:454-56.

INDEX